Did That Actually Happen?

About the Author

Paddy Duffy is a columnist and broadcaster from Donegal. He writes the weekly news review 'What Kind of Week Has It Been?' for the *Huffington Post* and is a regular commentator on RTÉ Radio 1's *Drivetime*. He has also written for the New York-based diaspora website IrishCentral.com and the European Youth Press, and has had work featured in *The Irish Times*, on the BBC, Al Jazeera and, most importantly, the *Donegal News*. He has also worked on TV shows such as *Top Gear* and *University Challenge*, and for nearly ten years he has been a youth worker, tutoring politics to young people as diverse as the Donegal Youth Council and doomed Political Science first years the day before an exam.

PADDY DUFFY

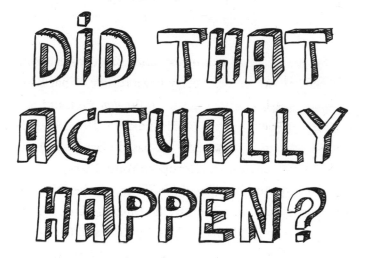

DID THAT ACTUALLY HAPPEN?

A Journey Through Ridiculous
Moments in Irish Politics

HACHETTE
BOOKS
IRELAND

First published in Ireland in 2013 by
HACHETTE BOOKS IRELAND

A CIP catalogue record for this book is available from the British
Library.

ISBN 978 1 4447 5041 6

Typeset in Plantin Light, Zap Bold and Univers Condensed by
Bookends Publishing Services

Printed and bound in Great Britain by
Clays Ltd, St Ives plc

Hachette Books Ireland policy is to use papers that are natural,
renewable and recyclable products and made from wood grown
in sustainable forests. The logging and manufacturing processes
are expected to conform to the environmental regulations of the
country of origin.

With thanks to *The Irish Times*, in which some of the images
first appeared.

Hachette Books Ireland
8 Castlecourt Centre, Castleknock, Dublin 15, Ireland
A division of Hachette UK Ltd
338 Euston Road, London NW1 3BH
www.hachette.ie

Dedicated to my family, and my students past, present and future of the Donegal Youth Council.

If they decide to do another book of this kind in forty years' time when you're all running everything, I am confident none of you will be in it.

'The Irish treat a serious thing as a joke, and a joke as a serious thing'

Sean O' Casey

'My way of joking is to tell the truth. It's the funniest joke in the world'

George Bernard Shaw

'That's fine in practice, but will it work in theory?'

Dr Garret Fitzgerald

'I don't normally do politics, but this government is an awful bollocks'

Bressie

Contents

They Went Where?!

Northern Exposure

Taoiseach's Questionables

The Epics

Introduction

Congratulations on buying this new book! I hope it's not too hard to assemble (it should come with the right number of screws and batteries) and it adds colour to your bookshelf/coffee table/bathroom.

In *Frasier*, Niles once claimed he dreamed of the day he could go to a library catalogue and see his name under mental illness. Like Dr Crane, I too dreamt of the day when I might see my name staring back at me in Easons, and it's scarcely believable that the day has come. Even scarcerly believabler is the way it came about.

Basically, this is all the newsreader Susanna Reid's fault. Because if I hadn't woken up one grey morning in Birmingham before work, and hadn't switched on the television, and hadn't seen Danny Healy-Rae on *BBC Breakfast* talking about drink-driving permits for the oul boys down the pub, then I likely wouldn't have looked out my window to see if blood was pouring from the heavens. I likely wouldn't have referenced it in my

'Drivetime' column on RTÉ the following week, and without that I likely wouldn't have been asked to write a book profiling some of the searingly unbelievable yet true stories of Irish politics.

The way I see it, politics is like *Emmerdale* with a lot more cash floating around. And only slightly fewer sheep. It may have a certain esoteric air about it, but politics too is filled with preposterous storylines, grave rivalries becoming strong friendships in the space of six months and vice versa, cartoonish villains and even the odd explosion. However much we try to intellectualise it, though, politics is fundamentally the study of people being people, people going mad with power (often literally) and getting into ludicrous scrapes. Ireland is the Shangri-la of such things.

In all seriousness, though, I've always felt that current affairs could stand to be dealt with differently. There is no godly reason why politics has to be dry, or dense, or disconnected from the rest of culture, because it's not. Hopefully some of the stories in this book, and the way they're presented, bear that out.

This book is far from exhaustive, but a compendium of stories I find to be indicative of the quirky, murky and the downright berserky Irish political landscape. I've tried to spread them round the years but have gravitated towards more recent tales because, well, have you seen the place recently?

For similar reasons, I've also not havered on stories or issues that have been covered extensively in other forms, for reasons of duplication and/or reader boredom. Lowry and phone licences or a Defence Minister calling the President a thundering disgrace? Old hat, man. Lowry planning to build a casino in the middle of nowhere and an Environment Minister having a sandwich thrown at him? That's more like it!

It also includes stories from the whole island. This isn't some sleekit way of trying to reintroduce Articles 2 and 3 or anything, but I figured given my own Ulster heritage it would be remiss of me not to.

I've also tried to subdue any political bias, although some people and some parties have a higher predilection for being hilarious than others. But I hope that in reading this book you will agree I've at least tried to be equally disparaging about all the political parties on the island. At the end of every story there is also a rating on various criteria, because 1) it's useful to break down the specific lunacy of these things sometimes, 2) both the publishers and I are big fans of *Strictly Come Dancing*. Please be advised that the scores contained herein are thoroughly haphazard and ultimately pointless.

Above all else, though, this is a humour book, or at least aims to be. It's not intended to be an academic treatise or a roadmap to recovery, but a look at the theatre of public life and the people who fill that stage, and who often fall into the orchestra pit.

I really hope you enjoy it.

Paddy Duffy
August 2013

How Do We Fare?

Enda Kenny is fond of repeating his wish that Ireland be the best small country in the world in which to do business (or BSCITWIWTDB, to give it its comically unwieldy acronym). But while Enda is intent on improving our business chops, there are plenty of things that Ireland punches above its weight in. Like punching, for example, as Ireland's Olympic record at boxing is pretty sterling. We're also pretty handy, proportional to our size, at churning out ace rugby stars, literary geniuses, people purporting to be Irish who've never been further east than Martha's Vineyard and, as this book should go some way to proving, abject political lunacy.

But is Ireland really that bad, in relative terms? Surely mad stuff happens in parliaments throughout the world, and it's only our proximity to events here that makes Ireland seem so particularly daft? Let's examine the evidence.

The United States

The US has a population about 50 times as big as ours, so naturally they should be able to bring 50 times the crazy to their political sphere. There is an extent to which that is true, as the US has the distinction of being the only country I can think of that had two vice presidents who shot people. Aaron Burr was the first, shooting former Secretary of the Treasury Alexander Hamilton in a duel (a bloody duel!) in 1804, while Dick Cheney shot his quail-hunting partner, elderly lawyer Harry Whittington, in the face at close range by accident in 2006. He still hasn't apologised. In fact, Harry apologised to Cheney for 'all he had to go through'.

You could fill a whole book about vice-presidential madness alone, in fact. Harry Truman was essentially tricked into becoming VP in 1944, when he was invited to listen in on a phone call President Roosevelt was having with his advisors informing him of Truman's uncertainty about taking the job. Truman heard FDR's best disappointed puppy-dog voice and duly took the post. Except little did Truman know that the whole conversation he was listening in on was completely staged to try and guilt him into running. He was elected VP in 1945, and became President a few months later.

Vice presidents are often a punch line but even the man in the big office can make laughable blunders, often in the most serious of situations. Jimmy Carter once left the nuclear codes in a suit that was being dry cleaned. When he became President and was given his nuclear briefing, the security advisor opened the doomsday briefcase to show Jimmy what was inside, and discovered someone had left an empty beer can and a condom in there as a joke.

But honourable mention goes to America's most ludicrous and yet awesome President, Theodore Roosevelt. This is a man who once reacted to being shot at point-blank range at a campaign rally by giving a speech 90 minutes long (the thickness of the speech in his pocket saved him, so it would have been rude not to read it after all that). For him, 'the nuclear launch codes' were probably the nicknames he gave his fists, and he used to love putting up his dukes with military aides to keep fit in the White House. One young charger gave him an almighty whack in the face, though, resulting in the loss of sight in his left eye. Philosophical to the end, he said in his autobiography, 'If it had been the right eye I should have been entirely unable to shoot. Accordingly I thought it better to acknowledge that I had become an elderly man and would have to stop boxing. I then took up jiu-jitsu for a few years.'

Hard. Core.

France

Ireland has a long tradition of politicians double, triple or even quadruple jobbing, but France takes that practice to strange new places. Take Martine Aubry, for example, leader of the Socialist Party and Mayor of Lille. Simultaneously. She became the Mayor in 2001, replacing Pierre Mauroy, who had been Lille's first citizen since 1973. As if being Mayor for 28 years wasn't enough, he also managed to be Prime Minister for three years and one of Francois Mitterand's closest allies. Nicolas Sarkozy also balanced being the Mayor of Neuilly with being a government minister, although he later became better known for his one-term presidency, his marriage to Carla Bruni and his alleged taking of big bundles of cash from the elderly heiress of the L'Oréal fashion house. It's a wonder how they fit it all in.

Brazil

Any candidate who has ever run for anything will tell you that to be a politician you need a seriously thick skin. What better candidate, then, than a rhino? Cacareco the rhinoceros was a candidate in the 1958 Sao Paolo City Council election, and although po-faced election officials didn't accept his candidacy, he garnered 100,000 votes, more than any of the main parties. Thirty years later, Tiao, described as 'a bad-tempered chimpanzee', was put up in Rio's mayoral election, and again humourless officials didn't count his votes. But it's estimated he would have come third if they did. Sort of puts Dustin's attempt at the presidency to shame.

Iceland

Sometimes, though, non-serious campaigns do end up getting taken quite seriously. Take the hubristically titled Best Party, founded by the comedian, actor and punk bassist Jón Gnarr. Frustrated by Iceland's political conflagration, Gnarr set up the party with a group of like-minded individuals who had no political experience whatsoever. Their first election, only months after foundation, was for Reykjavik City Council, and announced an 'anarcho-surrealist' 12-point manifesto that included, 'Free access to swimming pools for everyone and free towels: This is something that everyone should fall for, and it's the election promise we're most proud of' and 'Take those responsible for the economic collapse to court: Felt we had to include this.'

They won six out of 15 seats, making them the single biggest party on the council. But even when they were in the position to form a power-sharing agreement, The Best Party wasn't about to ditch its core idiosyncrasy just for power, and Jón Gnarr pledged to only coalesce with parties that had seen *The Wire*. His favourite character is Omar, apparently. While in office, he's dressed in drag for a Gay Pride parade, given a Christmas address while wearing a Darth Vader mask and Santa hat, and in a public discussion on Reddit revealed his favourite video games were 'Call of Duty, Half Life and Fruit Ninja in long meetings'.

Denmark

It's testimony to how well-adjusted Nordic countries are that even their gag candidates have a keener sense of civic duty than most of our regular ones. In 1994, after 15 years of trying, comedian Jacob Haugaard of the Union of Conscientiously Work-Shy Elements became an Independent member of the Folketing. This was an incredible achievement given the sparsity of non-aligned parliamentarians in Denmark's system of bounteous political parties, and also because he was a practical joke candidate who never actually thought he'd win and whose main election promise was to put Nutella in army field rations. Although he kept true to his comic self (he often wore shirts that looked like patchwork quilts and when asked who he would be supporting for a coalition government, he said, 'I didn't side with anyone, not even myself'), he did treat his (completely accidental) role and parliament with respect. While he never extracted demands for his home turf in exchange for votes like an Independent would here, he actually did manage to get Nutella in army rations.

The UK

Being the mother of all parliaments, most of the UK's political craziness comes from the centuries of tradition stacked up and up. Even one of the key positions in world politics, the role of Prime Minister, has been augmented and amended over time, like a constitutional game of Buckaroo.

In 1839 a young Queen Victoria invited one of the steadily more powerful PMs, Robert Peel, to form a Tory government. He said no problem, as long as Victoria sacked her chambermaids, who were all related to high-rolling Whig officials of the previous administration. Victoria told him where to go and asked Lord Melbourne to take over again, prompting what became known as the Bedchamber Crisis. Victorians were an innocent bunch.

In more recent times, prime ministers have had to deal with crises a bit less *Downton Abbey* in structure. Sir Alec Douglas Home, for example, foiled an attempted kidnapping at his friends' home just before the 1964 election. With his friends out and his bodyguard not in the house because there was no space for him, Sir Alec, 14th Earl of Home and thoroughly decent chap, eschewed the Liam Neeson method of conflict resolution with a much more soft-soap approach, reminding the left-wing students trying to lift him that if they did, the Tories would win a landslide. He also offered them beer. It worked. Prime ministers were never left quite so exposed again, but another step up in security took place in the early 1980s after the Brighton bombing. It didn't stop the IRA from launching a mortar attack on Downing Street in February 1991, though, and John Major (who wasn't the original target, as Margaret Thatcher was turfed out of office unexpectedly in November 1990 but hey, in for a penny, right?) responded to the almighty blast by emerging from under the table and saying to his cabinet, with surprising James Bond-esque sang-froid, 'I think we had better start again somewhere else.'

One of the UK's odd old political traditions has had a bit of an effect on Irish politics of late. In 2011 Gerry Adams wanted to run for a Dáil seat in Louth, meaning he would have to relinquish his Westminster seat for West Belfast. Except, he couldn't. Because the laws were established at a time when death was the only excuse for not seeing out your term, MPs can't technically resign. They instead have to step through a constitutional waiting room and take a notional paid position of the crown, the stewardship of the Chiltern Hundreds or the Manor of Northstead, to preclude them from being an MP. It's been done that way for hundreds of years, but lifelong Commons absentee Gerry Adams took exception, essentially saying it was stupid he had to pretend to look after a few fields just to get out of Westminster. Everyone else either laughed at the ludicrous quaintness of it all, or laughed at the republicans' republican having to take a crown position to leave the Queen's parliament.

South Korea

It may be better known for cars, futuristic technological capability and chubby-faced rappers miming horse racing, but South Korea has also become known as home to one of the world's scrappiest parliaments. *The Korea Times* ran an article titled 'Hall of Violence' that wrung its hands at the nation's legislature's increasing capacity for brawling, and with good reason. In 2004, as their President was being impeached, a full-scale ballroom blitz broke out, with punches and mahogany chests being thrown recklessly. One man crashed his jeep into parliament shouting, 'I'll kill you all.' In 2009 they were at it again, as Opposition members tried to storm a government committee meeting with sledgehammers and hoses. On the other side of the meeting-room doors, government reps, well ready for them, established a makeshift furniture barricade and, when they eventually broke through it, unleashed the fire extinguishers.

Italy

Ah, yes, the big kahuna of the bizarre political field. It's quite a feat that in a country that has had 40 prime ministers since the war, four of them have been Silvio Berlusconi. The owner of AC Milan and most of the commercial TV networks also had the longest continual run as PM since the war, at just shy of five years. Extraordinary, when you consider most Italian governments last as long as a special Director's Cut of *Gone with the Wind*.

It's even more extraordinary when you consider what an embarrassing lunatic Silvio is. In fact, a quick Google search of the words 'Silvio Berlusconi ridiculous disaster' will tell you all you need to know, but to give the highlights, he's been involved in massive conflicts of interest and incalculable court cases, appointed women to cabinet because he fancied them, held illicit bunga bunga parties involving minors, once claimed people should invest in Italy 'because we have many beautiful secretaries', said the victims of the L'Aquila earthquake should 'think of it as a camping trip', lionised Mussolini at a Holocaust memorial and referred to himself as 'the Jesus Christ of Italian politics'. He also had strippers dress up as Barack Obama for him. I could literally go on all year.

❖

So, is Ireland's political sphere really much more odd than all that? Well, read on …

They Said What?!

The Time Conor Lenihan
Advocated Specious Nonsense

Vive la difference isn't a bad motto by which to live your life. Of course, there are some people whose views on certain matters are so out there, so wilfully contrary, that the difference ends up pretty hard to live with: BNP'ers, Flat Earth'ers, Teabagg'ers, Climate Change Deny'ers, Kevin My'ers.

Also falling rather neatly into that category are anti-evolution theorists, who often have a view of the world so bizarrely simplistic, their argument itself sort of proves Darwin right.

Of course, as we learned with those PG Tips ads of the 1980s, you can dress pretty much anything up to look respectable. And so, John J. May tried to put an academic spin on the notion that we don't in fact share a provenance with monkeys, tea-making ones or otherwise.

He called it *The Origin of Specious Nonsense* (a pretty

good pun, in fairness to him), but even more of a coup than the title was who he got to launch the book: Conor Lenihan. Not just a sitting TD and member of one of Ireland's biggest political dynasties, but a junior minister. And not just a junior minister, but a junior minister for science. SCIENCE.

This was of course not remotely the first time Conor Lenihan (who also provided one of the All-Time Great

Ructions on Vincent Browne's show when he took exception to a question, lost the head and threatened to meet Vincent 'head on') had found himself in an embarrassing position completely counter to where he should have been. He achieved a certain notoriety when he said Joe Higgins should 'stick to the kebabs', a reference to Higgins' campaign for Turkish workers' rights. He was a junior minister at Foreign Affairs at the time. With special responsibility for Overseas Development and Human Rights.

Inevitably, such incongruity left people incredulous. The world-famous scientist P.Z. Myers, who had just been in Ireland on a lecture tour, expressed shock that a Minister for Science would lend such a book credibility. Lenihan's retort was two-pronged: a) he wasn't launching it as Minister for Science, but because the author was a constituent, and b) that just because he was launching it didn't necessarily mean he endorsed it. Clientelism or cognitive dissonance, take your pick!

In the end, May was so mortified at the shellacking that Lenihan took that he asked him not to launch the book after all, pointing specifically to his being 'eviscerated' on a political website. Much like everything else, the internet is a classic example of Survival of the Fittest.

❖

Perpetual Embarrassment Rating: 10/10

Conor Lenihan is the Usain Bolt of political mortification.

National Peril-o-meter: 5/10

Thankfully, Conor's innate ability for disaster means he's never too close to any red buttons.

'Ah, lads!' Rating: 9/10

It'd be like writing a book about modern medicine and getting it launched by a team of leeches.

Book title pun rating: 8/10

But Darwin probably beats him at everything else.

The Time the Healy-Rae Brothers Tried to Revolutionise Irish Transport

Daniel 'The Liberator' O'Connell, one of the greatest Irishmen who ever lived? He's one. J.B. Keane, pre-eminent wordsmith of his day? There's another one. Thomas Crean, intrepid adventurer and one-man snow plough? Him too. Hell, so was William Melville, the man who put the 'M' in MI5. As this list shows, some of the most distinguished Irish people have been Kerry people.

But, like a once razor-sharp comic making films where he plays 17 characters, all flatulent, Kerry's batting average of greats has gone down dramatically recently. Case in point: the Healy-Raes.

For years, Jackie, the Don Corleone of the outfit, was a rank-and-file Fianna Fáiler, helping candidates down the western seaboard get elected before getting himself on Kerry County Council in 1973. And it's in the local business he may well have stayed, until this 'supreme political strategist' was passed over for a place on the party General Election ticket in 1997. So he ran off his own steam instead, topped the poll, and became a disproportionate and terrifying influence on government until he retired in 2011.

Fast forward a decade and a half and with the Don of the family stepping down, that left his ladeens Danny (who, continuing the Sicilian metaphor, is Sonny) and Michael (who is, eh, Michael) leading the way. And taking after their Da, they weren't backward at coming forward with ideas for a brave new Ireland. First stop: number plates.

In February 2012, the freshman TD Michael Healy-Rae had a great idea to aid the Irish motor market, and ease the jitters of cash-flush triskaidekaphobes in one fell swoop, by suggesting cars sold the following year not bear the number 13. Hell, if they omit them from aeroplanes and Formula One cars, why not the everyday man's motor?

His logic, inevitably, was incredibly simple: 'People … are after going to the garages and saying they'll wait until the next year.'

Amazingly, number plates saying '131' or '132' actually ended up on our roads. Curiously, legislation concerning unbreakable wing mirrors, prohibiting black cat crossings or putting ladders on roof brackets didn't get nearly as far.

But the Healy-Rae ideas fan belt was only getting warmed up. With an innate sense for how to get attention that would rival Peter Mandelson, Danny Healy-Rae announced his novel idea for rural renewal in early 2013: let people drive half cut so they won't feel lonely. His suggestion was that '... gardai issue permits to persons living in rural isolated areas to allow them to drive home from their nearest pub, after having two or three drinks, on little-used roads, driving at very low speeds'.

He then added a gem of reductive psychology: 'This would greatly benefit people living alone looking at four walls and restore some bit of social activity in local pubs and may also help prevent depression and suicide.'

The fact that people just couldn't go down to the pub to meet the lads over a glass of Sprite being part of the problem seemed lost on him, as was the notion that the only safe way to negotiate rural roads at the best of times is by helicopter. Or indeed that the lack of public transport he lamented was precisely the sort of thing a county councillor like himself should amend. Though in fairness to him, it must have been hard to conceive of such notions when his media calendar was so busy.

The story was like tipping a supermarket meat counter into a piranha pool for the world media. Especially so when the politician in question looks like a man just home from a wedding in every photo ever taken of him. News stations in the US, Canada and Australia took the bait, as did four German stations, where Danny appears to have become the new Hasselhoff. The *Irish Examiner* reported that a filmmaker was making a (I can only imagine *Spinal Tap*-esque) documentary about him.

In an unlikely twist, he even got interviewed for German *Playboy*, and in a rather neat Irish tie-in Danny explained, with an apparent lack of knowledge about what the point of *Playboy* was: 'It was the one with Rosanna Davison in it. The one where she didn't have much on … I was further on in the magazine from her. I have three of the issues in the boot of the car, actually.'

In an interview with Susanna Reid on BBC TV Breakfast News, though, Danny was less impressive, starting the interview by referring to the show's 'listeners', a sure-fire way to prove you're a man with the head screwed on.

While news stations the world over were looking for a quote, back home people were trying desperately to shut him up. The Minister for Transport said he wasn't indifferent to the problem of social exclusion (which, knowing Leo Varadkar, was actually a bit of a surprise) but was adamant that 'the solution was neither alcohol nor drink driving'.

Alan Shatter put a similar kybosh on it, as did the head of the European Police Network, tersely stating, 'If you drink, don't drive, and if you drive, don't drink – it's as simple as that.'

The vast majority of the public may have either been

furious at the irresponsibility of the proposal or mortified by the gobdaw on international news, but according to Danny, sure the punters in Bally-Healy-Rae were loving it.

'The mobile hasn't stopped,' he said, although I wouldn't take bets as to whether he pulled over on the hard shoulder to take any of them. 'Most of the calls were supportive, though a few people, mainly from Dublin, were concerned about my views.'

Ah, yes, them busybodies up in Dublin, with their lattes and their buses every ten minutes. Sure what would they know about salt-of-the-earth laddybucks? They wouldn't have any concept of the concern the Healy-Raes have for social isolation in their area.

Oh, did I mention the Healy-Raes own a pub in Kilgarvan?

❖

Perpetual Embarrassment Rating: 10/10

If I need to explain why, you probably should put down your car keys.

National Peril-o-meter: 9/10

It's all fun and games until someone drunkenly drops their car keys down a gully outside the Healy-Rae pub, and then things'll backfire.

'Ah, lads!' Rating: 9/10

It's bad enough the whole world makes gags about our drunken incompetence on Saint Patrick's Day, without us having to endure this sort of thing in ordinary time.

What else do you suppose Danny has in his boot apart from *Playboy* editions?

I really don't want to know.

The Time Twink Nearly Made Fine Gael Die of Embarrassment

In 2013, John Bruton made something of a comeback. Enough time had passed that he was still able to remember his glory days on the field, but still felt he had something to contribute as a hurler on the ditch. And so, he spoke up on abortion law when his government stayed deathly silent on the matter, and spoke of the need for the public to tighten the belt and suck up austerity while sounding like a gout-ridden major in a Wilfred Owen poem. His own leadership of Fine Gael was of course far from perfect.

In 1991, Fine Gael were as fashionable as crushed velvet pantaloons. In the four years since they left power, Fine Gael treated leaders like a Hollywood getting changed montage. Garret with his professor look wouldn't do any more, then a formal Alan Dukes emerged but got the thumbs down too. Finally, a beaming

John Bruton stepped out, all flannel shirt and dungarees. A beleaguered party went, 'Feck it, that'll do.'

Being what Des O'Malley called 'a bull in a china shop', though, John Bruton was keenly aware of his image problem, a dinner dance man in an increasingly ravey world. Charles Haughey may have been like *House of Cards'* Francis Urquhart, but John Bruton was 100 per cent Frank Spencer.

To make over his image, Bruton brought in a hired gun: *Sharpe* writer and blunt political weapon, Eoghan Harris. He was just moving out of his red period (having hitherto been the doyen of the Workers' Party) and segueing into his blue period with Fine Gael (he'd later go a few shades darker with the Ulster Unionists). Long before he became bosom buddies with Bertie, Harris joined Fine Gael because of Bruton's 'highly passionate views' on Northern Ireland, and he was intent on getting the man into office. One commentator of the time said, 'If Harris can do it with that crew then he can title himself a genius.' Harris, you suspect, would readily accept that title.

With such palpable brilliance at the helm of Fine Gael's media strategy, what would Eoghan Harris do to bring Fine Gael into focus with an increasingly squinty public? Why, an American-style Árd Fheis featuring a tiresome comedienne making ribald jokes!

For reasons beyond all human understanding, comic relief for the event was provided by panto queen, zip expert and female Alan Partridge Adele King, aka Twink.

In character as Bernie the cleaner, she performed a sketch on stage replete with a massive picture of Bruton's face and the unfortunate slogan 'Fast Forward' all over the background. It was written by Harris (although Twink took credit for adding touches and timing), in which she made end-of-the-pier style jokes like Des O'Malley getting into bed with Charlie and then folding his arms and turning out the light, and seemed to intimate that she found John Bruton ferociously attractive. And also, 'a lovely boy who knew a lot about animals'.

Groucho Marx, it weren't.

Words were nothing, though, compared to the body language of Sean Barrett and John Bruton, who at various points inexplicably shared the stage with Bernie in full flow, and nearly cringed to death.

While the debacle is now remembered as a particularly embarrassing and lame attempt at political humour, the furore at the time revolved round Twink's reference to an incident involving Ned O'Keeffe and former RTÉ pol cor Una Claffey. To use Bernie's own words, Ned 'dropped the lámh' in the Dáil bar, before reciting a poem that went, 'Ned agus Una, Una gan gúna, Fianna Fáil gan Ned'.

Elizabeth Barrett Browning, it weren't.

Criticism came in thick and fast. Labour and the PDs condemned the use of a victim of an assault as a punch line, and *The Irish Times* reported that people were 'visibly uncomfortable'. One person in the audience was heard to joke, 'But apart from that Mrs Lincoln, what did you think of the play?'

His sketch as dead as Honest Abe, the papers were full of stories suggesting Harris might resign, or be asked to go. Clarifications abounded that Harris had nothing to do with Fine Gael policy or any of the non-Twink speeches made that night at the conference. A headline soon after read, 'Bruton did not vet Twink sketch', although he probably wished he'd neutered it before it ever saw the light of day.

Harris was typically bullish and defended the sketch, in particular the Una Gan Gúna debacle, with a typically daring strategy: 'The sketch was offensive and meant to be ... people couldn't cope with the new concept.'

Eh, OK.

He didn't stop there, claiming that 'a group of women journalists in particular' were waging a vendetta against him. 'I believe begrudgery is the reason for it, because Eoghan Harris has got too big for his boots,' said Eoghan Harris.

In spite of all that noise, Harris said he would go quietly (!) if he was asked, but added, 'I can tell you one thing – Fine Gael won't be at 23 per cent after the next election.'

He was right: they got 24.5 per cent.

John Bruton understandably told Harris to avoid public statements, but everyone else was just getting warmed up. An *Irish Times* report understatedly said the incident 'rather overshadowed the intention of the party leader'.

Alan Dukes was criticised for laughing on the night and criticising it in the cold light of day. One man wrote a letter to the editor suggesting Fine Gael set up a Twink Tank. And Twink herself, God bless her poor wit, maintained it was brilliant satire. The following year, *The Irish Times* ran the evocative headline 'Exorcising the ghost of Twink', which noted that for the '92 Árd Fheis, 'Eoghan Harris was in the front row but pulled no strings.'

In recent times, the sketch has been outdone in the embarrassment stakes by Clint Eastwood's one-man remake of *Frost/Nixon*. But, as his slight return to the news bears out, John Bruton hardly needs the help of Harris or Twink to embarrass himself.

❖

Perpetual Embarrassment Rating: 10/10
It's Twink. At a party conference. With cleaning products.

National Peril-o-meter: 2/10
It could have finished Fine Gael ... though that's hardly the same thing.

'Ah, lads!' Rating: 10/10
I repeat: TWINK AT A PARTY CONFERENCE.

Exorcising the ghost of Twink:
Took nine hours and five priests working in shifts.

The Time Michelle Mulherin Talked About the Birds and the Bees

Birds do it. Bees do it. Even educated fleas do it, although that opens up questions about the social mobility and opportunities of less-qualified members of the order *Siphonaptera*. The point is, everyone owes a great deal to sex; we all originate from the act of it, and afterwards we're either one or the other. But not everybody is quite so happy with the means of our provenance.

Over the years the list of people in Irish life who'd like to think we dropped from the sky like Mr Bean corresponds nicely to the list of people who've been in power. From the outset, the chances of the new nation being anything close to sexually liberated went out the window when the Committee of Evil Literature (!) got themselves an official stamp and gavel in 1926 and a remit to root out obscenity in all its forms. From then until the 1960s, even a quadruple entendre was verboten. Home-grown writers like Brendan Behan, John McGahern and Edna O'Brien and foreign mucky pups like Aldous Huxley and Balzac all failed the moral scrutineers. O'Brien came in for particular criticism from megalomaniacal Cavan cleric John Charles McQuaid, who described her book *The Lonely Girl* as 'particularly bad'. Which begs the question: how did he know how disgusting all this stuff was?

Even in the 1970s, where sideburns and flares ran wild, sex was still not a topic anyone in parliament wanted much to do with. When Mary Robinson proposed a contraception bill soon after joining the Seanad, she couldn't get so much as a seconder for the proposal. When a contraceptives bill eventually did go to the house in 1975, Taoiseach and world's sternest man Liam Cosgrave, along with eight of his party colleagues, voted against their own bloody government because he was so dead against the bill, and indeed dead against the pill. This was a time when women were smuggling in contraceptives on the train from Belfast to circumvent the ban. Ladies riding unaccompanied on a train was one thing, but carrying contraceptives was just a step too far. Incidentally, one of the Fine Gael members who voted against their own bloody bill was Oliver J. Flanagan, who became famous for his maxim that 'There was no sex in Ireland before television.'

Only in 1979 were contraceptives permitted in any sense, and only then for a man and wife so they wouldn't necessarily have 16 children if they didn't want to. The law was liberalised further in 1985, but not much further. When Virgin Megastores started selling condoms in 1991, legal moves were made against them, but all above the waist. The early 1990s were a bit of a *kulturkampf*, filled with pro-life protests, election leaflets that said things like 'Jobs for youth, not condoms' and generally large groups of people trying to keep Ireland in a world of crossroad dancing and the Bord na Móna theme. But try as they may, the sexy barbarians were at the gate.

In the mid-nineties, homosexuality and *Playboy* were both legalised, a kind of 7/10 split for cultural conservatives, and since then attitudes to sex and sex accessories has substantially liberalised. There are, however, some overhangs. Ladies and gentlemen, Michelle Mulherin, TD.

In April 2012, the Ringo of Fine Gael's Fab Four TDs in Mayo made a speech in the Dáil that will go down in public infamy, and will go down in the Oireachtas record, as is the usual procedure.

She began: 'I am against abortion in any form myself. The grace of God is so liberating and provides so many options to get the best out of life despite our fallen nature, and we all have that.'

Oh, hello, someone get the popcorn.

She continues: 'Abortion as murder, therefore sin, which is the religious argument, is no more sinful, from a scriptural point of view, than all other sins we don't legislate against, like greed, hate and fornication. The latter, being fornication, I would say, is probably the single most likely cause of unwanted pregnancies in this country.'

BINGO.

Inevitably, it was the use of the word 'fornication', a word going back to the days of Roman brothels and almost exclusively used by actresses like Miriam Margolyes playing uptight matrons in period dramas, that made people sit up and take notice.

Previous to this, Mulherin was best known for her proposal to reintroduce national service to counteract 'the culture of entitlement', and coupled with her surreal thoughts on the Libyan uprising ('The Libyan situation is an internal matter and coups and attempted coups are commonplace in Africa'), she was already marked out as something of an idiosyncratic old-style conservative. The fornication speech formed a holy trinity of news stories that set that perception in stone.

Explaining is losing, someone once said, and Michelle proceeded to explain all over the place. She also claimed to Matt Cooper that she was speaking honestly, 'rather than being clever about what I said', and nobody could ever accuse her of that.

❖

Perpetual Embarrassment Rating: 9/10
Amazing to think that Ireland still has a problem
with, ya know . . . the old S-E-X

National Peril-o-meter: 9/10
If we keep allowing fornication, we'll become a nation
of blaggards, cads and strumpets.

'Ah, lads!' Rating: 9/10
Maybe some day facts and logic and a grown-up
attitude will trump skewed morality in public and
government discourse, but not quite yet.

Best News Reaction Pun Award:
'Me So Forni'. Take a bow, Broadsheet.ie.

The Time a Councillor Said He Wouldn't Be Dealing with Them Blacks

Naas: it's a massive commuter town, and it has a lot going for it – some good pubs, some very nice restaurants, a courthouse, at least one good nightclub, and what appears to be a massive medicine ball in the middle of a roundabout. It even has some black people.

But in 2011, the Mayor of this town that embodies modern Irish life made a statement that belonged in a Bernard Manning set forty years ago, if it even belonged then.

Fine Gael's Darren Scully made the bold announcement that, after sustained run-ins with some rude people at his clinics, he was going to make a few changes and would be refusing to see black Africans.

Wait, what?

Yes, it turns out that during his clinics, Mayor Scully, who once had the campaign slogan 'A Fairer Ireland', found 'black Africans' to have bad manners and an aggressive attitude, and as such wasn't going to be dealing with them anymore. Funny, when black Africans are rude to politicians it's grounds for ignoring everyone from the continent, yet when white people do it, it's called talk radio. And yet, if Paul McGrath was signing a book in the local shop or Samantha Mumba was appearing at the aforementioned one good nightclub, he'd likely be over for a photo so fast he'd whack himself in the face with his Mayor chain.

Astonishingly, he made this statement on live radio, first on 4FM and then on local radio in Kildare, KFM, where the mystified presenter Clem Ryan saw a man in a hole and reach for a pneumatic drill.

He started by saying, 'First of all, my views and opinions by the way are my views and opinions. They do not represent Naas Town Council or Kildare County Council, or their views or policies.'

That's never a good sign. It's essentially code for: 'Even though I think what I'm saying is perfectly cool, the people I work for have run a bloody mile from it.' He goes on to describe his relationship with black Africans as 'not good', outlining various altercations, usually involving constituents getting shirty on housing issues.

At this point, any optimistic hope that 'Black Africans' is the name of one guy he has a problem with (like

Blackie Connors off *Glenroe*) and Scully has just been wildly misunderstood has gone out the window. But hey, if you're a Namibian of Dutch origin and live around the north Kildare area, you can rest easy.

He went on to etch permanent marker over his 'I'm not racist but ...' bingo card with phrases like, 'I have many non-national friends' and 'there's a taxi driver from an African country, I always engage in great craic, talking about football ...', 'I have lived abroad myself and I have embraced many, many cultures' and 'I watched *Guess Who's Coming To Dinner* once and I was totally on Sidney Poitier's side'.

Granted, I made the last one up, but it's no less ridiculous than the others.

When the presenter got down to brass tacks – claiming you're not a racist when you make a prejudicial

judgement of someone on the basis of their colour doesn't really stand up – Scully played a card just as potent as the race card: the white-man-just-saying-what-he-thinks card. Understandably, that card is often confused with the joker: 'I think, Clem, I've just ... as you well know me ... I do speak my mind and I do try and be very upfront with people.'

Unless of course you're from Sierra Leone, in which case he'll not be arsed. Although, when pressed on it further, he did concede the presenter's central point, yet divorced himself from it in a way that was vaguely impressive: 'I suppose, Clem, you could. I ... you know ... When you look up the word "racist" in the dictionary, yes you could probably say that it's wrong of me to make that decision but I'm only going purely on experience.'

There you go, racism is alright if you have a case study. Although, he did unwittingly reveal a loophole in his policy when pressed by Clem Ryan on the matter of someone calling him up: 'I don't know what colour anybody is over the telephone.'

A-ha! His genius scheme finally unravels! But for those black folk who tried to do it face to face, he had a very clear message: 'If any African comes to me in future, looking for me to make representations on their behalf, I'll politely introduce them to another councillor to deal with their query.'

So it's 'any African' now? Those Namibians weren't safe after all?! But after several minutes of statements that made the jaw drop, his final salvo was a real slap across the hollow cheek: 'But I'm only expressing my view and my opinion and I think that maybe in politics, that we should have a bit more of that, rather than playing it safe all the time.'

I know, right? Don't you hate those politicians who spend their time being respectful of the people they're supposed to be representing?

After the interview, the story exploded. A disconcerting amount of keyboard warriors weighed in with support with comments the likes of 'Dem Africans can't evin spell', but the general reaction was that of familiar dismay, with a slew of opinion articles castigating Scully with the general theme, 'Seriously? People are watching, lads!' Labour TD Aodhán Ó Ríordáin even made a complaint to the guards claiming he was inciting hatred.

Things went from bad to worse for Scully. He lost the mayoralty, and the Fine Gael whip. He tried the poor mouth card, white men over thirty being the most unfairly treated of any social group.

'Some people won't be happy til I'm deported,' he said with enough self-pity to bulldoze a high-rise apartment block. If he is deported, I hope the local representative in his new country is nice to him.

❖

Perpetual Embarrassment Rating: 9/10

You think you have the country just how you like it, then someone goes and racisms the place in front of everybody.

National Peril-o-meter: 5/10

Although it should be a lot higher, if you were to believe certain taxi drivers.

'Ah, lads!' Rating: 10/10

'I'm not racist, Clem, I just don't want to talk to someone because their skin colour is the same as a person who was rude to me once.'

Clem Ryan's saintly patience:

Apparently infinite.

The Time Fidelma Healy Eames Was Literally Living in a Parallel Universe

'I used to be with it, then they changed what "it" was, now what's "it" seems weird and scary to me.'

The Simpsons have a pertinent quote for every conceivable situation, and Abe 'Grandpa' Simpson's musings on pop culture describe with unswerving accuracy the up-to-dateness of Ireland's legislators. In fact, suggesting they used to be with it verges on the generous. But one Oireachtas head stands out for being comically, wilfully, spectacularly out of step with the modern world and all its wonders: Senator Fidelma Healy Eames.

To compound the Grandpa Simpson maxim, Fidelma also bears uncanny resemblance to Helen Lovejoy, wife of Springfield's Reverend, with her calling cry, 'Won't someone please think of the children!' Fidelma spends a lot of time thinking about the children, often with bewildering and hilarious results.

Her first foray into the world of technological innovation made young people the country over arch their eyebrows, like Roger Moore being told his car was being towed: she proposed 'some class of a microchip' that would switch a games console off after two hours, the sort of idea only a person who has never led a team to Champions League glory in a football manager game could come up with. Her crusade for healthy gaming practices for the nation's youth was, like all the best ideas, prompted by the inky reflex hammer of a solitary news story reporting an isolated incident of a young man who died of deep-vein thrombosis while playing absurdly long shifts on his Xbox.

But no sooner had the confusion-fuelled questions died down over her last initiative (What class of microchip is up for the job exactly? Could we not just circumvent the two-hour chip by switching it off after 90 minutes, taking a break for a wee bit, and then switch it on again? And isn't that what most people do anyway?) than Fidelma was thinking about the children again. This time, she had the internet in her sights. Or 'sites', as the kids seem to call them these days.

Speaking at the Oireachtas Committee on Social Media, Fidelma launched into a speech that was either a loving tribute to Molly Bloom's final chapter in *Ulysses* or proof that she gets her information about the internet from games of Chinese whispers held inside a whirling kaleidoscopic wind tunnel. 'Take for example,' she starts, 'the form called "fraping", where someone is raped on Facebook.'

Now while we can all agree that the phrase 'fraping' is horrible, Fidelma describes it with a definitive panache that misses the point as dramatically as those US missile defence shields that confused feet with inches. She also probably thinks that a news feed is a method of force-feeding kiddies junk food dressed up as recent developments, or that pressing the 'Like' button too many times would give you arthritis in real life.

She slightly redeemed herself by elaborating: 'Where a youngster has their status open and another person puts a message on there, as if they wrote it. And that message could be, for example, sexual. It goes out into the world as if they said it.'

That was a bit more like it, use of the word 'youngster' notwithstanding. But then, Fidelma being Fidelma, her brain just couldn't hold in her need to think of the children any longer: 'This type of thing has to stop. There has to be some controls put in place here. What about sexting? Where they are texting sexual images.'

Wake up, people! People are doing things online that may or may not be sexual! We need to ban this potentially sick filth! She then goes on to advocate a system similar to the Press Ombudsman (because the transnational internet is precisely like overseeing a few dozen newspapers in one country), stating: 'Until we have that, the public aren't going to be adequately educated or protected.' Fidelma herself serving as a case in point as to what happens when people aren't adequately educated about social media.

In a speech packed with more gems than a Jimi Hendrix album, it was her line about teenagers 'literally living in a parallel universe right now' that really caught the imagination. 'Literally living in a parallel universe', as if there are people like Sam Beckett in *Quantum Leap*, hopping dimensions, lurking behind doors and waiting for someone to leave the room without logging out to write something sexual on their Facebook.

And with that, Fidelma's bid to save the youngins from themselves based on phrases she appeared to hear just before walking into the committee chamber went viral. (This is where a disease spreads very rapidly on the internet.) But, as she may be aware due to her thoughts on IP addresses ('I am familiar with where IPs were registered in the United States and they couldn't be tracked down.' Nah, me neither.), a quick Google of her name will bear an impressive amount of fruit.

Stories like when a builder took a case against her for not paying the bill for the work he did on her gaff. The case was thrown out, but her husband still had to pay the man €12,000. Or the story where she was fined €1,850 for not paying her car tax. She wasn't there in person to collect the fine, though, as she was in the Seanad debating the Social Welfare Bill. And the story where she was fined €100 for travelling without a train ticket. At the time, a passenger claimed she got all 'Don't you know who I am?!' at the conductor who asked for her ticket. Fidelma strenuously denies that, but it's a mark of her esteem in Galway and the country at large that people found the passenger's version of events all too believable. Maybe there's a grain of truth in that notion that some of us are living in a parallel universe.

❖

Perpetual Embarrassment Rating: 9/10
Her own lack of embarrassment is balanced out by everyone else's.

National Peril-o-meter: 7/10
It's hard to know what's more dangerous: Fidelma in power or the VILE SEX BEASTS online.

'Ah, lads!' Rating: 9/10
You'd almost think elected representatives had no clue what they were talking about half the time, but just kept going anyway in a vain quest for importance.

Hyacinth Bucket rating:
A+

The Time Gerry Adams Wrote a Twitter Stream of Consciousness

As the old saying goes, 'Anyone who doesn't believe in miracles is not a realist.' That very much applies to Irish politics.

After all, what else is it but a miracle when a walking brimstone megaphone like Ian Paisley and the Bogside Art Garfunkel Martin McGuinness can live in harmony around a cabinet table after over four decades at each other's throats?

To that end, consider the case of Gerry Adams: as recently as the 1990s Gerry Adams was a media bogeyman. His face would be blacked out like a secretary being filmed on *The Cook Report* blowing the whistle on their money-laundering property developer boss. His statements would be read by Belfast actors (Sinn Féin voiceovers was one of the few growth industries in Northern Ireland at the time)

like Stephen Rea and, bizarrely enough, Paul Loughran, who played Butch Dingle on *Emmerdale*. Lynchpin satire of the 1990s *The Day Today* even pastiched the practice by having Steve Coogan appear on screen with a beard, Ulster accent and a vat of helium he had to inhale from to subtract credibility from his statements.

When he was finally allowed on screen, using his own voice, he wasn't exactly well received. When Gay Byrne had him on *The Late Late Show*, he refused to shake Adams' hand.

Since that time, Gerry's face and voice have become media mainstays, much to the chagrin of the Belfast actors' guild no doubt, and his deft ability as a speaker is either greatly admired or deeply resented, depending on your outlook. The rights and wrongs of Gerry Adams' political legacy will always be up for debate, but what is beyond dispute is that his Twitter page is bloody hilarious.

Over 30,000 follow Gerry's madcap antics on a daily basis, antics that are essentially a sitcom script 140 characters at a time. And like all good sitcoms, he has a great ensemble cast.

There's his dog Snowy, for starters, a very lovely Bichon Frise, and a more recent addition called Nuada (we know they're lovely because they feature in many Twitpics). He also has a teddy bear, called Ted. Ted features a great deal in Gerry's correspondence with the world, and seems to be a better-behaved Spit the Dog to Gerry's Bob Carolgees. Then there's some lad called Lightbulb, often alluded to but never seen, filling the 'Er Indoors/Maris/She Who Must Be Obeyed role.

But, above all else, what makes Gerry Adams' Twitter stream so compelling is the glorious banality of it. He cuts through the usual dry-balls political tweeting and just lets go in a jazz stylee. He'd go from making a serious political point to confessing he once brought a toothbrush into the Dáil because he thought it was a pen. Small wonder most people thought it was a piss-take to begin with.

But once people copped that it was legit, thousands flocked to see this hard-baked republican turn into a music-loving, pet-indulging surrealist softie. His musical taste was a particular revelation: his love of The Chieftains and Christy is far from surprising, but admitting to shedding a tear at a Joni Mitchell song and professing a love of Verdi and Vivaldi was positively revelatory.

Music aside, he offered thoughts on the types of things you would expect from the modern polymath, including food

> Porridge the JoeB way is with honey. And its spuds, cabbage, sweet potatoes, pot roast with tonsa garlic. Why am I tweeting about food?

washing habits

> In shower b4 Leaders after my bike ride. Water went off. Suds everywhere. Enda waiting. What2do? Nipped in2 bogs.Got sorted! Not myself since.

the Eurovision Song Contest

> When I was in Cage 11 in Long Kesh Gerard Rooney was there. He was a good friend of Bobby Sands. I c he is singing 4 Iceland. How cud that b?

and sport

> A great game of hurling on TG4. BAC v Luimnigh. Cluiche maith. Got 21 euro back on my big race bet. Minus my stake money we r 11 euro up. Yahoo!

Perhaps the most landmark story arc in Gerry's trance narrative was Ted becoming the fiancé of Tom, his bear life partner, proclaiming: 'Tom & Ted r officially engaged.

Congratulations 2 them both. Celebrations @ Teddy Bear Picnic Party later. Yippeee!' It was obviously a good party, as later on that night he tweeted:

> And so 2 bed. Party on going. But tá mise shattered.
> Tom&Ted ag shawaddying like Billyo, Whoever Billyo is! Time
> 4 zzzzz. Oiche mhaith daoibh.'

Fair play to them – the notion that 20 years ago Gerry Adams' two gay teddy bears could marry would have been unthinkable. On so very many levels.

❖

Perpetual Embarrassment Rating: 2/10
There's something quite joyous in Adams' complete lack of self-consciousness.

National Peril-o-meter: 5/10
Gay teddy bear marriage may tear the fabric of society apart, mind you.

'Ah, lads!' Rating: 6/10
I'll be honest, his love of Joni Mitchell totally threw me.

Any good tweets you left out earlier?
He said, '*Tiocfaidh ár latte*' at one stage. That was pretty good.

The Time Mary Coughlan
Lost at Science and Other Stuff Too

Ireland's a wonderful place. It's one of the very few countries in the world where any little girl can grow up to be a woefully inept second-in-command of the whole government. That's a level of social mobility we should be proud of. People in Raphoe, County Donegal were certainly proud when 'Congratulations, Mary' banners went up on the roadside. At first you'd be forgiven for thinking Mary was some local shopkeeper who'd turned 50, and a few hundred yards up the road you'd see pictures of her stapled to telegraph poles as a toddler, beaming a smile while sitting in a sink or something. But no, they were congratulating the fact that TD for the area Mary Coughlan was promoted to Tánaiste.

Her old school, the Ursuline Convent, was pleased too, as the *Sligo Champion* ran a classic 'Person from near here achieves something' local newspaper staple story. Apparently one of her friends remembered her as a bright spark and, with equal lucidity of recall, 'I remember her winning some award as the student of the year or something similar.'

On a national level, she had a reputation as a steady minister at Social Affairs and Agriculture, but within Donegal there was an undercurrent of bemusement to go with the pride of her cohorts. Mary Coughlan? As Tánaiste? Seriously? There's always a sense that Donegal gets under-represented when it comes to the big jobs, yet even with a Tánaiste from the county, there was a sense that Mary and under-representation would go hand in hand.

She wasn't just Tánaiste, though, she was also Minister for Enterprise, Trade and Innovation, and it was in this context that her reputation as the Derek Zoolander of the cabinet was sealed. At a meeting of entrepreneurs discussing the IDA's approach to promoting Ireland as a serious smart economy destination, she said the IDA would be promoting us as the innovation island, 'like Einstein explaining the Theory of Evolution'. What was that? A speech FOR ANTS?!

In fairness, the misappropriation of scientific theories was in reality no more stupid than the original simile. Surely if the IDA is trying to explain Ireland's innovation, they could have thought of a simpler concept to explain it than relativity? 'Business in Ireland: it's as easy as $E = MC^2$!'

Coughlan tried to sort-of laugh it off with a 'Yes, yes, I know who's who between Darwin and Einstein, we've all done Junior Cert Science,' but the damage was done. It wasn't helped by the fact that the same week in an Irish-language interview she referred to her coalition partners, the Green Party, not as Comhaontas Glas, but as Na Glasraí: the vegetables. Maybe she was conscious of cabinet leeks?

But that was just the tip of the iceberg. She was quietly sidelined during the Lisbon Treaty debate after not appearing to realise how many Commissioners the EU had, having made reference to the bigger countries having two. She made the comments in 2008, a full four years after the Commission numbers changed to accommodate the new accession states. She once claimed a cabinet meeting wouldn't be taking place that week, forgetting that not only had the cabinet convened the day before, but she led it in the Taoiseach's absence. The same day she was asked when the budget would be, and she replied that it was up to the cabinet to decide the date of the election, a Freudian slip that put the rumour mill into overdrive.

But when she wasn't nearly accidentally dissolving the Dáil, she was also at odds with her cabinet colleagues. She criticised An Bord Snip Nua for their proposals not making any sense, which brought sharp criticism from the Department of Finance. She claimed she was in talks with Ryanair over their hated Airport Tax, but the Department of Finance contradicted her again. And she allowed the former Director of FÁS Roddy Molloy to get away with an exorbitant pension, and then topped it up later on, leading to a massive fight over who was to blame with Finance Minister Brian Lenihan nearly forcing her to resign.

As a result of all those, plus blasé comments like, 'I think the type of emigration that we have … It's the type of people that have left have gone on the basis that … they want to enjoy themselves' and bizarro ones like, 'We would like to revert back to the international reputation we had and continue to have', the Tánaiste became the lightning rod for all government criticism. 'Calamity Coughlan' picked up more alter egos than David Bowie, names like 'Typhoid Mary' for her capacity to spread gaffes around, or indeed 'Blunder Woman', or indeed 'Sweary Mary' for her bullish and earthy attitude to, well, pretty much everything, from IDA officials to local constituents.

Eventually, with her unforced errors reaching dangerously high levels and her abrasive manner doing her no favours with a beleaguered public, it became increasingly likely that her perpetually safe seat was under serious threat. The die seemed cast when Sinn Féin hotshoe Pearse Doherty launched a broadside at her in the Dáil during his maiden speech, when a disengaged Coughlan was heckling him in between checking her phone. By the time the election came around, she was nowhere in the hunt for the final seat.

But Mary Zoolander, showing that there's more to life

than being really, really, really ridiculously unsuited to high office, re-imagined herself as that highest of beings on the earth right now: reality TV judge. On TG4's *Feirm Factor*. Her biog on the website contains some amusingly unnecessary quotation marks referencing her work in the Department of Agriculture on issues such as 'Bird Flu' and 'Foot and Mouth Disease'. They didn't put the one thing that actually would have deserved quotation marks, though: 'Tánaiste'.

❖

Perpetual Embarrassment Rating: 10/10
Seriously?

National Peril-o-meter: 9/10
Only two things genuinely put a chill up my spine: remembering my driving test and momentarily forgetting that I passed it, and the notion that Mary Coughlan may have been Taoiseach.

'Ah, lads!' Rating: 9/10
Not only was she nearly Taoiseach, but she was Minister for Education. She was actually in charge of teaching kids to read good.

Mary's favourite swear word:
I hear it's '*&%*@sticks'.

The Time Pee Flynn
Went to the Zoo on Live TV

In the summer of 1977, as disco music was reaching its peak, a vainglorious, cavalier, bombastic man in a white suit strutted down the street and into notoriety. No, not Tony Manero from *Saturday Night Fever*, but Pádraig Flynn from Castlebar. On his first day in the Dáil.

With an uncanny talent for getting noticed (people in Castlebar would often comment on his habit of turning up slightly but ostentatiously late for Mass and proceeding to walk all the way up to the front for a seat), he became one of Haughey's prominent loyalists and balcony guards during the many attempts to defenestrate him.

He was a key minister when Charles Haughey called the most pointless election ever in 1989, a mere two years after coming to power. Flynn was one of the main advocates of a snap poll for several reasons: 1) it would be a good way to raise some money for the Fianna Fáil war chest, 2) there was a good chance the party could win a much-coveted overall majority, 3) it would be a good chance to raise some money, 4) it would knock the hated PDs off their perch and 5) dude, seriously, it would be a good way to raise money. The election was a huge mistake and Fianna Fáil actually lost four seats, but their money-raising was much more successful. Flynn managed to get £50,000 from Sligo-born developer Tom Gilmartin. More on that anon.

Flynn was a vocal opponent of the family reunion that history has come to know as the Fianna Fáil–PD coalition (prompted by their election stunt), calling it a dereliction of their core values, whatever they are. Haughey ploughed on ahead anyway, and tension between the two men bubbled under. Having lost all confidence in Haughey by 1991, he realised there was space for only one rampant egotist in the party, and backed the country and western revolution in 1992, saying 'Pee Flynn would be doing himself a disservice' if he didn't.

It served him pretty well, and he became Minister for Justice, then Industry and Commerce, before being pushed upstairs to the European Commission.

It was while wearing that hat that Pee rocked up on *The Late Late Show* in 1999. Gay Byrne, fully aware of the fact that he was dealing with the most indiscreet man in Christendom, lathered on the 'Pee, me oul china, me oul sundown, me oul mucker!', praising his 'aplomb' in

Brussels. Boy did it work, as he went on to completely aplomb himself. He was on to talk about the scandal-riddled Santer Commission, but Pee, with his penchant for the phrase 'I wanna tell ya somethin' ...', proceeded to do just that.

The most notorious bit of course is where he outlined his hard-knock, three-house life on £100,000 a year and to try it some time, making every mouth in the country a makeshift fly trap. When Gay asked about what his lifestyle might be like after Brussels, he said he 'did have a few pensions that you [looking out at the audience] are paying for'. Nice of him to notice, I guess.

Another notorious section of the interview was when he referred to his daughter Beverley, the only time where Pee used the Flynn name that wasn't a third-person reference to himself. 'She'd leave me standing, as a politician,' he claimed, also calling her 'a class act'. If by 'class' he meant 'advising bank customers to illegally invest in offshore schemes', then she was arguably the classiest woman alive.

His dramatic defence of his daughter and matter-of-fact money talk have endured in popular culture, but it was his Olympic-standard aspersion casting of Tom Gilmartin that proved to have the most lasting effect. In classic style he started off with, 'I ain't saying anymore on that, except to say ...'

He should have quit while he was ahead. He said he hadn't seen Gilmartin for years, but that his bid for

business in Dublin didn't work out for him and that he wasn't well, that his wife wasn't well, and that he was 'out of sorts'. At the end of the interview, which had exceeded the time allocated, Gay said to him, 'You've run me over!' Gilmartin felt the same.

Watching on Tara Television in Luton, Gilmartin, who had hitherto disengaged from the Flood Tribunal investigating corrupt payments, was suddenly spurred to action, as he wanted to dispel the notion that 'he was some kind of looney out to destroy Dublin'. This is perhaps the first time someone has ever given evidence to a judge because something on the TV pissed them off.

Gilmartin duly testified, and several things emerged. You may want to sit down for this. The £50,000 Gilmartin gave Flynn for Fianna Fáil ended up being used for Pee's own personal use. Better still, Bertie Ahern knew about the payment the year it was made, but didn't ask Flynn about it until a decade later. Gilmartin also claimed Flynn asked him to lie about the payment at the tribunal. Probably most damning of all was the *raison d'être* behind the payment. Gilmartin had come to the realisation, aided by the advice of Owen O'Callaghan (a successful businessman who Gilmartin once saw fall out of a broom cupboard while eavesdropping on a meeting, because things weren't ridiculous enough to begin with), that to get anywhere in Irish business, politicians had to be bought. Flynn may have had a penchant for Travolta suits back in the day, but in 1989 it seemed greased was the word.

In 2012, a mere 13 years after Pee's televised peacocking, the by then Mahon Tribunal found Flynn to have 'wrongly and corruptly' taken the payment. With a move by Lisa Chambers, Castlebar's newest hotshoe Fianna Fáil candidate, to expel him in the offing, Pádraig Flynn resigned from the party. His first appearance in public after the expulsion, as it goes, was in Mass in Castlebar. Not sure whether he was on time or at the front, though.

❖

Perpetual Embarrassment Rating: 1/10
Another of our growing 'no shame' pile.

National Peril-o-meter: 8/10
If you're willing to needlessly risk being cast to the Opposition benches for a few extra seats and a good bit of extra bob, God knows what else you'd do.

'Ah, lads!' Rating: 9/10
What would he not have said on *The Late Late* if Gay had been passing him whiskey or something?

Who would play him in a Hollywood movie?
The only man who could play Pee Flynn is Pee Flynn. Although I'd love to see Kevin Spacey give it a go.

The Time Ned O'Keeffe Thought a Talking Pig Would Be Bad for Business

As we've established an embarrassing number of times, the Irish electorate will forgive literally anything as long as their representative is seen to do good by the parish. But there are some instances where a TD's actions are just so weird that you really wonder how. Ladies and gentlemen, Mr Ned O'Keeffe.

For nearly 30 years, and in seven elections, the good people of Cork East comfortably returned Ned to the Dáil. He managed to do this despite having racked up a prodigiously insane list of public statements.

Apart from being a TD, Ned was also the highest-profile pig farmer in the country, at least before the film *Snatch* was released anyway. In 1995 he claimed *Babe*, that nice old film about a pig who wants to boss sheep around and rodents who think they're Frankie Valli, should be banned. Why? Because he feared having a cute anthropomorphic piglet on our screens might affect sales of Christmas ham. And that just won't do, pig.

Ned's concern for butchers' livelihoods wasn't the first time he displayed a lack of (heh) gammon sense when it came to matters of pigriculture. In 2000, Labour tabled a motion proposing to ban bone meal as a source of nutrition for farm animals, as bone meal was thought to be a reason behind the outbreak of BSE. Ned O'Keeffe voted against the motion, but neglected to declare his quite large interest in the matter: he was one of just 17 licensees in the whole country that made bone meal. He was also, inevitably, a junior minister at the Department of Agriculture at the time with special responsibility for food safety. That didn't last long.

But it would be unfair of me to focus in on Ned's pig-related gaffes and eccentricities. Especially when he has so many more of them on so many other topics.

Ned was the man at the centre of the 'Una Gan Gúna' affair, where he groped the RTÉ political correspondent Una Claffey in the Dáil bar. Twink made several 'oo-er missus' references to it at the 'Kill it! Kill it with fire!' Fine Gael Árd Fheis in 1991 (see *The Time Twink Nearly Made Fine Gael Die of Embarrassment*).

In recent years, with no more elections to run, he let his public comments go jazz fusion. Consider this expert treatise on Ireland's financial situation on local Cork radio:

'The blame for the problems we have is nothing to do

with the banks, it is down purely and simply to politicians, the planners and the county councils. We have a foreigner in place telling us we should sell our banks and I don't want the Chinese coming in here.'

The foreigner jibe was a reference to Matthew Elderfield, the Cambridge-educated financial regulator who— Hold on, what was that about the Chinese?! He elucidated, if that's the right word:

> We had 800 years of English rule; if we let the Chinese in and give them a base here like they have in the Sudan and in other parts of Africa, then where will we be? They would then probably take over the place with military bases and so on.

But Ned also reckons if the Chinese don't take over, the Irish Defence Forces definitely will. 'Our political system is going to fail further ... and I see the real possibility of an army coup.'

If they did, he'd probably take credit for the jobs in Kilworth Barracks outside Fermoy. For what it's worth, the Defence Forces released a statement that they '... serve the State every day of every year and we don't involve ourselves in political matters', which is of course exactly what they'd say if they were planning a coup but didn't want anyone to know.

The outburst didn't exactly help his son Kevin, who was out canvassing to replace him while Ned outlined his coup d'état theory. Kevin said, 'I'll leave him to his own. I'm shocked. He can shoot away,' which is probably the last thing he should do under a military junta.

Whatever his thoughts on the Chinese or military takeover, he didn't seem to be all that enamoured with the people in office at the time either. He diagnosed the Fianna Fáil–Green coalition's fundamental problem: they were much too intelligent. He reasoned there were 'too many intellectuals and too many people from outside business' in government, the clear implication being it could really have done with the odd pig farmer knocking round.

He then asked, 'Who there in cabinet ever bought a bale of hay?' It must surely rank up there with 'Where's the beef?' in the greatest all-time agriculture-themed political questions.

But it would be unfair of me to merely cast Ned O'Keeffe as some kind of arch-eccentric. He was hypocritical too. He fulminated about NAMA, but voted for it anyway, explaining, 'I've always taken the party pledge.' Except when he didn't take the pledge, losing the whip by voting no confidence in Mary Harney as Health Minister.

He also blasted Fianna Fáil's thrall to Agha Khan wannabe high rollers: 'Fianna Fáil went wrong when it became the party of the racehorse owner.' In spite of this he also had a lot of time for Charles Haughey, racehorse owner. 'So what if Charlie liked nice women and a few extra nice shirts? He was the best leader we ever had.'

But it would be unfair of me to merely cast Ned

O'Keeffe as some kind of hypocrite. He was a terrible local representative too. He once told a lobby group trying to get a proper school building in Rathcormac that he wouldn't be lobbying for them because 'There is a fabulous layout of Portakabins there.'

It gets better, though, as he explained how Rathcormac, palatial prefabs aside, wasn't a priority for him because he didn't get many votes there in the 2007 election. 'Why should I look after the people of Rathcormac if they didn't look after me?' he asked.

Full marks for honesty, I guess.

❖

Perpetual Embarrassment Rating: 9/10
Probably a bit more if you're Kevin O'Keeffe.

National Peril-o-meter: 9/10
An army coup deposed by the Chinese, and nobody eating pork. It's a bloody nightmare.

'Ah, lads!' Rating: 9/10
I'm looking very forward to the next series of *A Portakabin in the Sun* with Phil and Kirsty.

Hay-giarchy:
A government of people with experience in matters of baling hay.

The Time Voters Were Told
an Atheist Opposition Leader
Beat His Mass-going Kids

Essentially, modern Irish politics started in 1948. Following 16 years of unbroken rule, Fianna Fáil's Opposition in the Dáil resolved to put their many, many differences behind them and form a penta-partite coalition government (with a few Independents to boot), for, as the old saying goes, 'The enemy of my enemy would make an OK Minister for External Affairs.'

But apart from setting the template that would govern Ireland for decades (two parts Fianna Fáil, one part coalition of parties that would never sit together anywhere else in Europe), the 1948 election did much more besides. It kicked in motion the regular cycle of new parties bursting onto the scene, before exploding. It introduced new policies and new methods of campaigning. And it also brought some real lows in negative campaigning.

The first election of the modern age was one that was actually called in haste. Fianna Fáil were plagued by torpor, economic woe and corruption (stop me if you think you've heard this one before). The decision to call the election was prompted by a discussion between Éamon 'Long Fellow' de Valera and Seán 'Is Mise' Lemass, who supposedly told Dev, 'You are not the man I think you are if the Dáil is not dissolved before I get back.'

I then like to imagine that they did a windmill handshake like in *Top Gun*.

The snap election called by the Maverick and Goose of Irish politics was in the main to head off the challenge from the emerging Iceman, Sean MacBride. Son of an Easter Rising martyr and W.B. Yeats' daydream fantasy Maud Gonne, and former Chief of Staff of the IRA in his own right, his Clann na Poblachta party was republican, progressive and fresh, in other words everything Fianna Fáil were in 1932 when they took power. And precisely because of this, Fianna Fáil hated them.

At every turnabout, with no apparent irony that they had been victims of similar epithets only 16 years hither, Clann na Poblachta were branded by Fianna Fáil as dangerous communist atheists. At one point in Bray, a reverend mother was telling people that MacBride didn't just not believe in God, but beat his faithful kids for going to Mass. The Clann meanwhile were putting their Godless liberal minds to new ways of reaching the public that didn't involve stepping on a box, instead spending megabucks on a pioneering promotional 15-minute film called *Our Country*. In the end, though, all that fancy fillum-makin' didn't do them that much good, as the meat and two veg voters of the country found the Clann a bit spicy for their taste.

At one point pundits were suggesting they could win 75 seats and an overall majority, but whether due to the scare tactics or good old-fashioned Irish fickleness for anything even slightly different, their vote was nowhere near where predicted, and they ended up with a mere ten.

Fianna Fáil, despite being lousy with scandal and public frustration, was still the top party and only lost eight seats (before 2011, losing eight seats was considered a really bad day at the office for Fianna Fáil; see *The Time Fianna Fáil Exploded*), but they were miles away from forming a government by themselves, as back in those days Fianna Fáil didn't cohabit. And so, armed with nothing but favourable maths and hate in their heart for de Valera, the motleyest crew of parties that ever resolved to coalesce came together: the gentlemen lawyers and curtain salesmen of Fine Gael, the supposedly Communist-ridden Labour Party, the supposedly Communist-free National Labour Party who hated the other Labour Party's breathing guts, the humble farm boys of Clann na Talmhan, and brash but chastened Clann na Poblachta. They were backed by a collection of Independents, the kind of out-there eccentrics and lunatics that would come to be a regular feature of Irish politics. People like James Dillon, the only man in the Dáil to argue against wartime neutrality and who shut down his family pub because too many men were spending their wages in there, and Ollie Flanagan, a Papal Knight who could never find a problem the Jews and liberals weren't responsible for.

But even though they had the numbers, they then had to get a man to lead them who would appeal to a government that was conservative, socialist, republican, West Brit, arch-Catholic, uber-Protestant, urbane and rural all at once. Fine Gael's leader and ex-army general Richard Mulcahy was the natural choice as leader of the biggest party, but his appointment was vetoed by MacBride, who as a former 'RA chief would have made him as comfortable as being stuck in a lift with W.B. Yeats. With civil war discord threatening to unravel the government even before it took office, they turned to John A. Costello, the essence of inoffensive. He had so little baggage from the revolutionary era, the only interaction he had with the Easter Rising was being stuck at a barricade in his car after a day at Portmarnock Golf Club.

The Costello-led first Inter-Party Government lasted for nearly three years, in that time overseeing the establishment of the Republic and all but eradicating tuberculosis. But it was the outrageous plan to give a mother and her child free State healthcare that was the smoking gun that blew the government apart.

Costello's famous reaction to the scheme, following immense pressure from both the medical and clerical professions, was that he was 'A Catholic first and an Irishman second'. Dr Noël Browne resigned in disgust, but interestingly his party leader, that dangerous atheist Sean MacBride, backed Costello. Bet that nun in Bray felt awful embarrassed after that.

❖

Perpetual Embarrassment Rating: 5/10
Surprisingly little, although Ollie Flanagan could go off at any minute.

National Peril-o-meter: 2/10
Fianna Fáil may have warned of the dangers of coalition and socialism and God knows what else, but neither the coalition nor Clann na Poblachta caused the nation too much damage. They couldn't say the same about themselves, though.

'Ah, lads!' Rating: 9/10
A nun telling barefaced lies for political advantage? That'd need a few rosaries said to walk that one off.

Best slogan of the election campaign:
A popular cigarette company of the day imploring people to 'Vote Early, Vote Afton'.

The Time a Green
TD Turned the Air Blue

Shane McEntee seemed to sense something on 11 December 2009 in the Dáil, as when discussing that year's Social Welfare Bill, he said, 'I ask Deputy Gogarty not to fly off the handle.' Easier said than done.

Gogo was under pressure. He was a backbench member of the Green Party in league with Fianna Fáil, an increasingly tilty windmill in an economic tornado. He didn't like voting for the punishing things the government was doing but he would do it anyway, even if he once said education cuts made him want to 'vomit continuously'. The few deputies in the Dáil that were there at that time sensed they had a shaky suspect, so they shone a lamp in his face hoping he might crack.

Deputy McEntee first gave it a go, calling Gogarty a champion of schools and that 'He knows how they will be hit ... I ask Deputy Gogarty to stand up to it. He knows right from wrong.' Oof.

Joe Costello was the next to give the heartstrings a pluck. 'I appeal to these Members to realise that it is not too late. Deputy Gogarty … I would hope will either abstain or vote against this.'

Gogarty got up to speak, but the Opposition wasn't done. 'Deputy Gogarty should do the right thing,' said Roisin Shorthall, adding her voice to the three-part Opposition harmony.

At this stage one Emmet Stagg got in on the argument, an argument he will now forever be part of. 'Always blathering,' he chimed, while Shorthall smelled blood. 'Does Deputy Gogarty not think the wealthy should pay their share?' They didn't seem to realise that when you provoke a Green, he might turn into a hulk.

Gogo pleaded, 'I respected the Deputy's sincerity and I ask him to respect mine.'

Stagg, unaware a heavy mist was descending, hit back: 'The Deputy does not seem very sincere, from what he has been saying.'

And then it happened – the swear heard round the world: 'With all due respect, in the most unparliamentary language, FUCK YOU, DEPUTY STAGG! FUCK YOU! I apologise now for my use of unparliamentary language.'

Gogo had gone Full Alan Partridge, and that was his 'smell my cheese' moment.

It wasn't his first bizarre public outburst (he once mimed a fit and then played dead as a kind of tableau while Frances Fitzgerald discussed incinerators at a public meeting) but it was by far the biggest. Within minutes the video was online, and not long after that came OYR (Obligatory YouTube Remixes). Even *Have I Got News For You* profiled it, making him the Fuck You Deputy Stagg Guy forever more. So started the sensational pilot in a disturbingly compelling series of *The Unfortunate Adventures of Gogo*.

He may have been a punch line but he was in good company, as the Greens had only slightly more credibility than David Icke or Jim Corr at this point. Their situation was summed up by a press conference held in November 2010 calling for an election. There seated in a line, like the Reservoir Dogs but all called Mr Green, were Messrs Gormley, Boyle, Sargent, Ó Brolcháin, Cuffe, a teddy bear, Gogarty and his toddler daughter Daisy. Wait, what?!

He explained that since the presser was called at short notice he had no babysitter and had no recourse, but the image of an 18-month-old up there with a government parliamentary party spoke for itself.

That and other incidents made him a popular topic on Twitter, where his political notoriety made him a key figure. Except, he developed a habit for locking people out, as he got shirty with and blocked numerous high-profile critics and punters alike.

He put Twitter to good use though on election day, when he became not just the first person to concede, but the first person to concede online. He decided to leave politics 'with good grace', but what would he do next? Hey, this is Gogo, what wouldn't he do?

The first thing he did post-politics he actually did while still vying for the seat, being one of the faces of *The Naked Election* documentary on RTÉ. The documentary profiled his pathos-riddled campaign that lacked a director, his love of The Human League, and his old chat-up line where he claimed he was '25 percent gay, so heterosexual with a twist' ('I was a niche market,' he laughed, as his wife walks past with a look on her face that screamed, 'You're telling me').

His next episode was as manager of Oughterard GAA team for RTÉ's *Celebrity Bainisteoir*. Traditionally, when the manager walks into the dressing room, a monster 'Wahey, it's Calum Best!' sort of cheer goes up. But when Gogo walked in, there was only deadly silence. Once they figured out this guy was the manager and their hopes of getting Rosanna Davison or whoever were officially scuppered, they rallied and gave him a courtesy cheer. Some of the team twigged who he was after Fuck You, Deputy Stagg was invoked.

The New Romantic manager turned to music in August 2012 when he, like Kirk Van Houten from *The Simpsons*, recorded his own song, 'Wishing on a Photograph', trading under the name His Sweet Surprise (sure why not?). He also recorded an accompanying video, easily one of the maddest things ever conceived. Selected highlights include him looking through photos in a Jacob's USA biscuits box, getting abducted at a cake sale, getting shot in the face, attending his own funeral in ghost form and discovering the officiating priest killed him, who goes on to shift the face off one of the mourners. The video ends with him being plied with drink by a witch before finding himself on a beach. It was like falling asleep during a David Lynch film after eating a wheel of cheese.

In 2013 he released an EP, a play-to-the-gallery tune called 'Radio' he hopes is Eurovision-worthy. Anyone tempted to throw a 'don't quit the day job' jibe his way should know the local Oughterard Fianna Fáil branch wanted him to stand.

❖

Perpetual Embarrassment Rating: 10/10
I have no need to expand on that, surely?

National Peril-o-meter: 8/10
What sort of world are we living in when a man can be kidnapped at a cake sale in his own video?

'Ah, lads!' Rating: 9/10
Swearing in parliament is not cool. Mind you, if he had given an impassioned speech on school funding, he would never have appeared on *Have I Got News For You*.

Chances of Paul Gogarty appearing in a new series of *Twin Peaks*:
It would be remiss of David Lynch not to include him.

The Time Phil Hogan Charged Us to Deal with Our Shite

A new government, they said. No more arrogant incompetence, they said. It'll be grand, they said!

In fairness, anyone with political knowledge beyond seeing episodes of *The West Wing* would have known deep down that a Fine Gael/Labour coalition making a radical shift in policy from Fianna Fáil, especially in the Augean stables that is our economy, was a flight of folly. But what a lot of people did hope was that the style of government might change. A Fine Gael/Labour coalition, after fourteen chastening long years on the Opposition benches, would surely be in a position to lead a more compassionate, connected, trustworthy and upbeat government.

Nah.

Far and away the biggest mood killer in the cabinet is

Big Phil Hogan. With all the charm of hired muscle in an episode of *The Sweeney*, it appears to be Phil's job to give the public a few swift punches to the bread basket, and anyone who complains gets a curt 'Leave it, you slag!'

It may have seemed impossible, but Phil Hogan probably rivals the likes of Michael McDowell and Dick Roche in the love-to-hate ministerial stakes. At St Patrick's Day in Kilkenny in 2012, someone 'threw half a ham sandwich (with brown sauce on it) that narrowly missed him'. Throwing deli meats at someone in Kilkenny, it seems, is on a cultural par to throwing shoes in Iraq. Just as well there wasn't Brie in it, or someone could have been killed. According to the *Kilkenny People* report, 'Gardaí are investigating how the culprit managed to miss the two very tall men.'

Meat wasn't the only way people showed their dislike. His website, featuring a photo of Phil with his jacket jauntily launched over his shoulder, was hacked, and he was roundly booed at a Kilkenny hurling event. So what exactly had he done for such a landfill of opprobrium? Let me count the ways.

Maybe it's the photo of him in Doha being wined and dined on the week of the budget. Or maybe it was how he 'completely traumatised' an old woman. John Bruton's former private secretary Anne O'Connell said to him at a golf outing that she hoped he wouldn't 'screw property owners'. He replied, 'I have no problem screwing you. Hasn't Máirtín [her husband] been screwing you for years?'

He apparently gave her an apology on a 'scribbled note'.

Or maybe it was his letter assuring a neighbourhood in Kilkenny that it would not be getting a Traveller family moving in near them, raising roars of racism and abuse of power. Or maybe it was his text to a woman who told him of her concern for children going hungry in the country responding: 'Would u ever relax. And feed the children.' Feed the children, brilliant, why didn't she think of that?

But even though he appeared to conscientiously be as brutish and distant as possible, his legislative to-do list hardly helped. As Minister for the Environment, it fell to him to literally hit people where they live, being the all-too-gleeful frontman for the property tax and septic tank charge. The septic tank issue, inevitably, caused quite a stink.

Even with European directives and the need to ensure clean water standards as his shield, Hurricane Phil still nearly sparked an agrarian revolt by announcing a mandatory inspection of septic tanks. Fast becoming a symbol of the government's supposed intention to tax shoelaces, shaving cream and everything in between, GIT OFF MA LAWN! types didn't take kindly to the notion of paying £50 to have an official poking round their septic tank like Gillian McKeith. Even with a discounted offer of £5 and a grant scheme to update any tanks needing work, he still had a problem getting people to comply. But if folk thought Hogan was giving them unnecessary crap over their septic tanks, it was small beer compared to the household charge/property tax, which has turned him into a modern-day Lord Trevelyan.

Of all the issues affecting this government's popularity, the decision to tax people's homes was probably the most contentious. Enda Kenny himself called it immoral back in the nineties, but hey, a lot of things have gone by the wayside since then, like bomber jackets and runners with lights in the heel. Phil Hogan's love of a registration spreadsheet and a good scrap with the public meant he was the natural choice to be the frontman for the household charge. There were ructions.

Oscillating from poor organisation to tough-guy threats, and with 'Can't pay, won't pay' a common refrain around the country, the front man couldn't seem to get anyone singing the same tune. With nobody in cabinet exactly sure how or where the charge could be paid (there was an extended and embarrassing thinking out loud in public about whether you could pay it at the Post Office), or indeed even when the final deadline was. 'Basically, it's a shambles', summated RTÉ's Brian Dowling.

But like a substitute teacher with zero authority, it wasn't long before Hogan was disproportionately lashing out, only making everyone laugh all the more. He invoked the spirit of Malcolm X by advocating 'any means necessary' to collecting the household charge, and fully endorsed Clare County Council's decision to withhold college grants to students if their parents didn't pay it. More hilarious still, Hogan then suggested door-to-door personal reminders by council staffers of non-payers, presumably rolling round neighbourhoods in open-top Land Rovers, chanting threats through megaphones and swinging bags of doorknobs to put the wind up people. Better still, to give the whole story a bit of a tree-in-the-hole-and-the-hole-in-the-bog feel, council staff were warned that if they didn't warn people about how they'd be in trouble if they didn't pay, they too would be in trouble.

With the charge for an unpopular charge being led by an unpopular man, you'd think a rather drastic rethink in attitude wouldn't go amiss. Not so for Big Phil. At the height of the controversy it emerged Phil himself hadn't paid service charges of his own, on his apartment in the Algarve, to the tune of €4,320. 'Why would you pay a charge if you were unhappy with the service?' he asked. Finally, he gets it.

❖

Perpetual Embarrassment Rating: 10/10

I have no need to expand on that, surely?

National Peril-o-meter: 7/10

The country might just fall into the sea if people don't cough up for their house. I can't imagine his seat is all that safe either.

'Ah, lads!' Rating: 9/10

To call him a bull in a china shop is to discredit bovine manners.

A trip to Doha?

It must have been for a Qatar-ly report. High-o!

They Did What?!

The Time Aengus
Ó Snodaigh Hoarded a
Pile of Ink

In 2009 the British parliament was consumed by an expenses crisis. It seemed everyone had their hand in the till, which, given the 650 MPs at Westminster, made for a bloody big till. Some of the more big-ticket articles have become legendary: the duck houses, the kinky films, the housing flips. It seemed nobody was safe, with ministers resigning and backbenchers being convicted all over the shop.

In early 2012, Ireland had a bit of an expenses furore of its own: Sinn Féin TD Aengus Ó Snodaigh hoarded a big pile of ink. And by 'big', I mean '50 grand's worth'. He amassed this bill over the space of two years, using 434 cartridges, enough apparently to send 3.25 million letters. It would have been cheaper to buy a couple of hundred octopi and just milk them.

Given how Sinn Féin make a substantial virtue of their hair shirt attitude to taking public money, the sheer oddness of using nearly two industrial wages in ink cartridges made for quite an eye-catching story. Especially so for the impish wags in the press and Twitter, as they found that Irish republicanism and printing was a surprisingly fruitful ground for puns, Ó Snodaigh being rechristened 'Wolfe Toner' and song lyrics changed to 'Come out ye blackened hands'.

In response to the rather fair question 'What were you doing with all that ink?', a mortified Ó Snodaigh explained to Rachael English of RTÉ (which showed footage of someone printing something off on a Windows 95 computer in their news package, in case nobody knew how that happened) that he was 'well known as a prolific leafer', which sounds like the sort of thing that could get you arrested if you weren't careful. A better answer would have been, 'I've been swimming in it, Rachael. It works wonders for the oul pores,' but that would have been unlikely to diffuse the tension.

Rachael also added that since the clampdown on such expenses largely prompted by him (which surely must have prompted feelings of pride in a 'Because of me they have a sign' sort of way), he still owed nearly €4,000. Ó Snodaigh said he was getting round to paying it.

The reaction to Aengus seemingly producing his own copy of *Vanity Fair* for the people of Dublin South

Central was pretty much what you'd expect. Within his own party Mary Lou McDonald made it as a contender for understatement of the year when she said 50 grand on ink was 'a bit excessive'. Meanwhile Micheál Martin, with the nerve of a bomb disposal expert, demanded an investigation by the Oireachtas Commission.

Since the black (and yellow, cyan and magenta) days of 2007 and 2008, Aengus seems to have toned it down (heh) a bit, and he's probably learned to just give the ink a good hard shake and put it back in again. And even though it was embarrassing for a while, it must be a relief for him that we're in a place now in politics where we can mention 'Sinn Féin' and 'cartridges' in a jokey context.

❖

Perpetual Embarrassment Rating: 7/10
Somehow, it's actually more embarrassing that he spent that much money on something work-related than if he'd spent it on something decadent like, say, slankets.

National Peril-o-meter: 8/10
What if one of his ink smudges got on the Constitution, and changed the meaning of a paragraph entirely? That could totally have happened.

'Ah, lads!' Rating: 7/10

Hopefully Aengus has a more ink-efficient printer now that does a few more sheets to the gallon.

The rate of business at the Bluebell branch of Deco's World of Printers since the new rules came in:

Disappointingly slow.

The Time an Auctioneer Sang for Votes

As has been said in another chapter (see *The Time a Council Meeting Discussed Eminem*), music and politics are inextricably linked. Not just in the Christy Moore sense, but songs expressly used for electioneering purposes have been a pivotal part of politics for years all over the world. In the United States you had 'Happy Days Are Here Again' for FDR, Frank Sinatra singing 'High Hopes' for JFK, to say nothing of the infuriatingly catchy 'Kennedy Kennedy Ken-ne-dy for Me' jingle, or more recently Bill Clinton's use of Fleetwood Mac's 'Don't Stop' and Barack Obama's favourite, U2's 'City of Blinding Lights'.

Closer to home, Labour's use of 'Things Can Only Get Better' has come to represent the New Labour product as a whole, and even closerer to home Colm 'C.T.' Wilkinson, the original Jean Valjean (could you imagine Hugh Jackman singing a campaign song for the Australian Liberals? I personally really don't want to), really gave it socks singing 'Your Kind of Country' for Fianna Fáil in 1977. Labour's director of elections blasted it, though, saying, 'I've liked pop music all my life and I don't even like the lyrics.'

But more recently, we've had an auctioneer with a perm.

In 2007, Clara man John Bracken was facing an uphill battle to get a seat in Laois/Offaly. He was an Independent in a constituency boasting then Finance Minister Brian Cowen and he had large coat-tails, a strong Fine Gael presence led by frontbencher Olwyn Enright, as well as Tom Parlon for the PDs. So for him to stand half a chance, he was going to need something big. He was going to need a song.

And boy did he pull it out of the bag. A jaunty number typical of that you'd hear on a local radio early afternoon show incorporating both musical genres – country and western – the song (main lyric: 'Sure he's your only man!') plus Bracken's posters of him with impeccably coiffured hair and shirt with the top two buttons perilously unbuttoned caught the national imagination. Unfortunately for him, the notoriety didn't translate to votes, as he got just shy of a thousand number ones. He bounced back for the local elections in 2009 with another dootsy sort of dinner-dance tune, with the opening line 'Do you remember John Bracken?' With just 3 per cent of the votes, the answer appeared to be no.

South Tipperary TD (and a man who looks like he'd be handy at a pub darts tournament) Mattie McGrath wasn't to be outdone, and released a similarly barnstorming (emphasis on the barn) campaign song of his own for 2011, the lyrics of the chorus, 'Toor-ay-yah, Mattie McGrath, our guy, your guy, Mattie McGraaaaaath!', proving atonally hypnotising. The spell is broken almost immediately though in the next line, with a heinous crime against rhyming couplets: 'Mattie is the people's choice, put him in the Dáil, won't that be nice?' Ivor Novello it ain't. Meanwhile, watching the video is an experience in itself, effectively a slideshow of Mattie's greatest poses (Mattie in hat, Mattie at a school with his mayoral chain, Mattie looking tough with his shades on, etc) book-ended by an ident for the film maker involving the chaotically photoshopped head of a young ginger boy at the start, and a crudely formatted campaign poster at the end for over a minute, once the glamour shots had finished. Because of – or perhaps in spite of – all this, Mattie continues to be the people's choice, whether it rhymes with anything or not.

As you may have spotted by now, this kind of thing seems to be generally tried with the good honest rural dinner-in-the-middle-of-the-day folk of the country, and maintaining this paradigm was former Irish Farmers'

Association President John Dillon, who released a campaign song for his run for election in Limerick in 2011. His was quite a different proposition from the others, though, in that it was quite good. A rockabilly-style number containing shades of Eddie Cochran and backing singers reminiscent of the Plastic Ono Band, the lyrics were also quite entertaining: 'Well I lost my job and I'm on the dole, the bank man says you're out on your hole' and '... a country boy with loads of muscle, who's going to bring the fight to Brussels'. Beautiful. Alas though he never got to go to Brussels; he was put out on his hole, only getting 10 per cent of the vote.

And last (and also in fact least), campaign songs aren't just limited to domestic campaigns, and in 2009 someone posted a song and accompanying video for Galway's answer to Citizen Kane Declan Ganley's failed attempt to go to Brussels. It contained lyrics, sang to the tune 'I'll Tell Me Ma', like 'He is clever, he is witty, he has read the Lisbon Treaty!' It's unlikely Declan Ganley had anything to do with this song. Although given how bad it is, even if he did he probably wouldn't admit it.

❖

Perpetual Embarrassment Rating: 9/10
How about we make a deal: politicians stop making records, and we'll stop Bono going on about politics, yeah?

National Peril-o-meter: 4/10

Maybe some day some evil genius will devise a tune to brainwash us, Pied Piper style, and assume control of the country. But it won't be an auctioneer from Offaly.

'Ah, lads!' Rating: 9/10

'Toor-ay-yah, Mattie McGrath' is Boney M-esque in its antiquated earworm bona fides.

Suggested collaborators for John Bracken's next election song:

Kraftwerk.

The Time a Man
Painted Brian Cowen
on the Toilet

There are many things in life that you hope you will never have to see: war, natural disasters, Twink on *The Late Late Show*. But perhaps above all else, the one thing you would never wish to see is the headline 'Naked taoiseach paintings removed' on the BBC News website. Not that them being removed wasn't a relief, mind.

From early in his premiership, Brian Cowen developed an uncanny talent for being at the centre of unnecessarily embarrassing news stories. But unlike his decision to go on air sounding like Darth Vader (see *The Time Everyone Suspected Brian Cowen Drank the Lakes of Pontchartrain Dry*) or paint himself into a constitutional corner (see *The Time the Government Nearly Made Itself Illegal*), it was the reactions of his over-zealous staff that made for the problems here.

It all kicked off when schoolteacher and renegade artist Conor Casby did a reverse heist and actually put paintings in two galleries, the Royal Hibernian and the National Gallery. If you were thinking Conor is some kind of suave Peter O'Toole type, going round being impish and artsy with Audrey Hepburn or some such, that image is shattered when you realise that the paintings Casby was adding both involved nude Brian Cowen, one of him clutching underpants, the other a toilet roll. I say nude – he was at least wearing his glasses. The sainted Audrey would never have anything to do with bogroll or keks.

The paintings didn't last on the wall long, but pictures of the picture spread like wildfire. As you might expect when an artist sneaks into prestigious galleries and hangs two nudie pictures of the head of government, it got a bit of media attention. RTÉ News did a knowing report on the painting, even getting an auctioneer in to assess them. And that's when a harmless 'And finally ...' on a single news bulletin became noted in posterity on *Reeling in the Years*, and necessitated a Wikipedia page titled 'Brian Cowen nude portraits controversy'.

The following night on the nine o'clock news, RTÉ folded like a well-made Swedish bed settee as Eileen Dunne made an overblown apology at the end of the bulletin. To this day, the RTÉ article online about the incident contains the preamble:

On the twenty-third of March 2009 Nine News, we carried a report on the illicit hanging of caricatures

of the Taoiseach in two Dublin galleries. RTÉ News
would like to apologise for any personal offence caused
to Mr Cowen or his family or for any disrespect
shown to the office of Taoiseach by our broadcast.

I do wonder what 'illicit hanging' actually means. Placing them at a jaunty angle? It turned out that Cowen's press secretary, acting on his own initiative, had made a complaint to RTÉ. He took particular offence at the 'oversensational' timbre of the tongue-in-cheek report, and the line where the reporter claimed it was uncertain if Cowen posed for the artist. He wasn't the only one, as others such as Fianna Fáil TD Michael Kennedy chipped in, suggesting RTÉ's Director General consider his position. Seanad leader Donie Cassidy said it was a sick joke, and as an ex-showband promoter he ought to know a little bit about dodgy artistic vision. Predictably prim One Man Seminary Senator Ronan Mullen said the media was abusing Cowen's personal dignity, which I suppose was generous of him to suggest Cowen had any left.

Things only got worse when the dragnet was laid over Today FM, as *Ray D'Arcy Show* producer Will Hanafin revealed on air that the (at the time) anonymous artist had been in contact, first through a friend and then directly once the whole thing blew up. At this stage the DPP had prepared a file on the case (?!) and the guards came to the station to quiz Hanafin and asked for the details of the correspondence, which Hanafin refused. The guard responded that he could obtain a warrant to search any

such emails, and that he had been given direction 'from on high to investigate'. A warrant. To search for a rogue painter of nude caricatures.

Hanafin wasn't the only one to find the whole thing crazy. Enda Kenny decried RTÉ's grovelling apology, Labour's Liz McManus bigged up the need for satire in Irish life, while Frances Fitzgerald and David Norris, no stranger to caricature himself, said the whole thing was completely over the top. Joan Burton probably made the best point at all, saying that embarrassing as it might have been for the Cowen family, it took six months for an investigation to be launched into Anglo Irish Bank. The public also found their voice on the matter, with a Facebook group titled 'Leave Conor Casby Alone!' gaining considerable support.

Casby, as it goes, was indeed eventually left alone, hoping to draw a line under it by selling the paintings for charity. Meanwhile, as the whole debacle died down, Brian Cowen, who to his credit had kept above the indignity of the whole thing, knew all too well that an easel, a gallery or a sarcastic news report were the least of his worries.

❖

Perpetual Embarrassment Rating: 8/10
It should have been a bit embarrassing for Cowen, but it was the reaction from everyone else that was really shameful.

National Peril-o-meter: 2/10
Unless the walls of the galleries themselves are surreptitious pieces of priceless art, negligible.

'Ah, lads!' Rating: 9/10
Cops going to a radio producer and asking for emails of a mystery painter of political nudes. It's just like an episode of *The Wire*.

Silliness felt by Eileen Dunne reading out that apology:
Palpable, I imagine.

The Time a Glass Che Guevara Nearly Took Over Galway

Galway is one of the greatest places on the planet. It's a city that acts like a village, a non-conformist, non-compliant cultural haven, a cobbled paradise on the weather-beaten Atlantic coast. So attractive is it that it's often nicknamed 'the graveyard of ambition', as once people fall victim to its charms, they never want to do anything anywhere else.

If Che Guevara hadn't been killed in Bolivia he would have no doubt moved to Galway, the home of his Lynch ancestors, in due course. He would have had a great time, bumming round the Spanish Arch with a bottle of Bucky, spared the harbour chill by a German army surplus jacket. Galway city councillor Billy Cameron thought so, and he proposed a monument on Salthill promenade.

In recent times, cities all round the world making

monuments of modern heroes is very much in vogue. In Cambridge, they have a bust of King of Nature David Attenborough on the grounds of his old Uni stomping ground, Clare College. In downtown Milwaukee, they have a statue of Arthur Fonzarelli which they call 'The Bronze Fonz', and in Detroit they've just built a bronze statue of Robocop. Robocop.

You might think that Galway could hardly go weirder than a bronze Robocop, but if you think that, you just don't know Galway. Because what Billy Cameron was proposing was a monument to Che that was made of glass. And five metres high.

The artist's impression of the Che monument was, eh, interesting, with Jim Fitzpatrick's iconic T-shirt design rendered through clear and blue-tinted glass, with a red background. Five metres high. Billy Cameron also claimed the (five-metre high) monument would be jointly funded by the Cuban and Argentine embassies and suggested it would put Galway on the map with an explanation more salesman than socialist: 'To associate yourself with the [Che] brand you are immediately getting the added value.'

God knows why or how, but word of the monument spread to Ileana Ros-Lehtinen, Chairperson of the Foreign Relations Committee for the US House of Representatives. Crucially though, she's also Havana-born and represents Florida's 27th congressional district that takes in Miami, an area where Castro and Co. aren't terribly well thought of. Even so, with humanitarian disaster in Syria, nuclear menace in North Korea, the long end of a longer war in Afghanistan, and sanctioning Palestine for getting all uppity with their impertinent bid to become a country, she managed to find time to give a letter to Enda Kenny about a monument that hadn't even been built yet, in a city with a population about the tenth the size of her constituency on the other side of the ocean.

She was joined in her criticism of the dedication to whom she called 'a mass murderer and human rights abuser' by Galway resident and Tony Stark wannabe Declan Ganley (sure who else?). With all the moderation of a man wearing a sandwich board saying the world will end this Friday, he sounded off:

'Galway should not risk its reputation, its image, its future, and its deep links with the United States by allowing this offensive monument to be built in our city,' he said. 'It will drive away tourism, jeopardise investment, and leave us all the poorer.'

And reduce Galway's annual good weather quota to a fortnight too, probably.

Continuing the dramatic diagnosis, he added, 'It would be a monument to the insensitivity and ignorance of those who dreamt it up, and it would shame the people of Galway and Ireland.'

Given his appropriation of the Easter Rising in his election literature in the past (see *The Time Photoshopping*

Referendum Posters Became a Craze), Guevara was obviously one freedom fighter too far for Ganley.

The comically disproportionate furore didn't end there. Lawrence J. Haas, Al Gore's former press secretary, hand-wrung to high heavens asking if the monument to a 'homicidal maniac' suggested our moral compass was shot to hell, in a piece bewilderingly titled 'Che-worship infects the land of shamrocks'. The magnificently named Yale historian Carlos Eire waded in by comparing Guevara to Hitler and Cromwell (the double whammy!). Even the *New York Times'* superstar columnist Maureen Dowd covered the whole kerfuffle.

In the end, the firestorm was extinguished by slabber. With so much global heat being thrown at a bit of (admittedly quite tall) glass in Salthill, Hildegarde Naughton, Mayor of Galway city, claimed that while she voted in favour of a motion honouring Che, she didn't realise there was a monument involved.

This is the same Hildegarde Naughton who denied David Norris a hearing of endorsement for the city council because she didn't realise what she was voting for then either (see *The Time a Whole Pile of People Wanted to Live in the Zoo*). 'There was no reference to a monument in the notice of motion we voted in favour of,' she claimed, adding, 'As a democrat, I cannot support the placing of a monument in memory of Che Guevara in our city.'

Which makes you wonder why she voted in favour of

the motion in the first place. A mystified Billy Cameron asked, 'What did they think we were going to have – an egg and spoon race for Che Guevara?'

The idea hasn't been revived since early 2012 but if Cameron ever wanted to he'd do well to take the lead of the Galway Democratic Republic, a mystery group of guerilla pranksters the likes of which could only exist in the west. They created a stir by placing a series of plaques at the Spanish Arch over a couple of weeks, including one commemorating 'Any future victims of the nation's space exploration programme'. The motto at the bottom of every plaque, raised by the acronym-friendly Society for Historical Interpretation, Trusteeship and Education (prompting an actual local headline 'Concern over SHITE erection'), stated '*Ita erat quando hic adveni*', Latin for 'It was like that when I got here'. A conservative message even Ros-Lehtinen and Ganley could get on board with.

❖

Perpetual Embarrassment Rating: 7/10

Hildegarde Naughton's habit for not knowing what she's voting for is getting embarrassing.

National Peril-o-meter: 5/10

Ganley's histrionics aside, the worst that was likely to happen was a heavy brow-beating. Which we sort of got.

'Ah, lads!' Rating: 5/10

Ludicrous though it was, by Galway standards it's pretty tame. Stand-up arguments on socialist iconography happen pretty much every night, like.

The Ron Burgundy 'Wow, that escalated fast!' award:

How the hell did leading American columnists, politicians and academics catch on to it so quickly? Is there some kind of Che bell they can all hear?

The Time
Fianna Fáil Exploded

As Bruce Willis films or those demolition shows on obscure satellite channels pay regular testimony to, everybody likes to see things blow up. And possibly no explosion has ever rippled through the national sinews more satisfyingly than the one that took place in February 2011. For that was when Fianna Fáil were destroyed with such systematic brutality, Quentin Tarantino would've felt woozy.

The crudely scrawled graffiti was on the wall for ages, as Fianna Fáil created and then dealt with a catastrophe of Jurassic Park levels. They knew it too, and a significant number of FF top brass dived overboard rather than have the public push them off the plank. Of the 39 TDs who retired before the 2011 election, 24 of them were in the outgoing government, about a third of the parliamentary party. As if that wasn't portentous enough, Fianna Fáil were fielding fewer candidates than ever before in the vain hope it might shore up their vote. Running a sole candidate in constituencies where they had two TDs was a sure-fire sign that the Soldiers of Destiny were fated for doom.

In spite of all the signs, though, plenty of people still thought the ever-resourceful Fianna Fáil would somehow survive their nuclear winter, that Fianna Fáil could only be truly defeated if decapitated in a swordfight at the top of a mountain. But something happened for all those 'believe it when I see it' people on 26 February: they got to see it.

The first signs of disaster came that morning where an exit poll suggested the party were polling around 8 per cent in Dublin, a number that when extrapolated meant Fianna Fáil would be able to count their capital TDs on their thumbs. As results poured in, Fianna Fáil TDs started tumbling comically, like a scene in Adam West-era *Batman*. John Curran? Blammo! Pat Carey? Pow! Michael Mulcahy? Oof!

Both Dublin North TDs, Michael Kennedy and Darragh O'Brien, were put to their Swords, while Mr Tallaght, Charlie O'Connor, was stripped of his title after losing two thirds of his vote. Conor Lenihan lost his seat in the same constituency, but he couldn't have kept his seat with a moat, portcullis and force field. And in Dún Laoghaire, two high-profile ministers, Mary Hanafin and Barry Andrews, also conceited defeat. Sorry, conceded defeat, ahem. But despite their bonfire in Dublin, nowhere demonstrated the rot better than Limerick city. It too possessed two big-name TDs, Willie O'Dea and Peter Power. Willie (see *The Time Willie O'Dea Pulled Out His Strap and Laid Some Busters Down*) was a former cabinet minister renowned for majorities most other politicians would have to register whole pet cemeteries to get, and for being 35 per cent moustache. Peter Power was seen – at least by himself – as an up-and-comer and had been appointed FF's Foreign Affairs spokesman before the election. Although the role had about as much force or effect as a man down the pub going, 'Jesus, isn't this thing in Syria desperate?'

The Fianna Fáil ticket went from 24,042 votes in 2007 to a desultory 9,259 four years later. Willie's uber-human tally was cut by 23 per cent and he suffered the humiliation of waiting six counts. To put that in perspective, the last time he hadn't been elected on the first count was 24 November 1982. Fittingly, the number one on that day was Eddy Grant's 'I Don't Wanna Dance'. It was worse for Power, as with Willie's massive coattails taken in severely he didn't even last til the sixth count, knocked out in the fifth with a mere 5 per cent of the vote.

All over the country there were similar stories, with long-established Fianna Fáil TDs looking vulnerable, and not in the way that made people want to mother them. In 1997 when the Tories were booted out of power, the highlight of the night was arguably the 'Portillo moment', when Michael Portillo (prior to his days when travelling on trains and the like rehabilitated his reputation) was widely considered to be a bit of a git, and everyone took immense *Schadenfreude* in his defeat. But with FF seat losses by the dozen all over the country, the Portillo moments were stacked on several levels, like a good tin of biscuits.

But also like a tin of biscuits, a few favourites will always emerge, and in this case the best fillings were Dick Roche, who went from being Ireland's representative on *Newsnight* to crashing out six counts before the end of the election, losing 7,000 votes in the process. There was Mary Coughlan, at one stage one heartbeat away from being leader of the country (a notion which nearly gave us all a heart attack), who lost half her votes, and everybody's respect. And let's not forget Martin Mansergh, Fianna Fáil's last angry man (at least when Vincent Browne interviewed him), who once told an inquisitive Fine Gael senator to 'respect your betters'! What sweet irony then that he would miss out on a seat to Mattie McGrath. And then miss out on a Seanad seat because he only got nine votes.

The prat de resistance though was undoubtedly John O'Donoghue, who launched into a 'People Who Really Fecked Me Over' speech of pompous hilarity. 'I hope that the irony will not be lost upon you, that I stand here on my evening of defeat, in a hall, this magnificent sports complex, which I helped to build.'

You sensed that if he could have, he'd have done a

Ray Burke (see *The Time Ray Burke Pulled Up Trees out of Spite*) and pulled the hall out of its foundations, just to show the ingrates what's what.

When the dust settled, Fianna Fáil were left with 20 seats, a number that near put them with O'Leary in the grave. On the day, a pundit on RTÉ said Fianna Fáil would have to become a niche party. Interior decorating maybe?

❖

Perpetual Embarrassment Rating: 10/10
John O'Donoghue alone would max out this score, in fairness.

National Peril-o-meter: 3/10
Fianna Fáilers may think they are the country, but frankly, having them out of office was the safest thing for everyone.

'Ah, lads!' Rating: 7/10
Seriously like, John O'Donoghue ... the state of him ...

Comeuppance-ness: 10/10
If electoral *Schadenfreude* is wrong, then I don't want to be right. It was like a Portillo moment, drenched in chocolate and caramel.

The Time Fine Gael Plotted against Their Leader Really Badly

In February 2011, Enda Kenny was elected Taoiseach. He was joined in the top-tier government positions by Health Minister James Reilly, Finance Minister Michael Noonan and Justice Minister Alan Shatter. But it could have all been so very different.

Seven years after he promised to electrify the party, Enda Kenny's leadership of Fine Gael was in dire need of a few jolts. A poll in June 2010 had Enda Kenny and Fine Gael trailing an effervescent Labour and an ailing Fianna Fáil in the polls, and only mildly more popular than diabetes. Brian Cowen's government was on the ropes, yet the only card Enda seemed to have was calling continuous no-confidence motions that had no hope in passing. His handling of George Lee in the parliamentary party was widely criticised too (see *The Time George Lee Paid a Flying Visit to the Dáil*).

With an election seemingly no more than a year away, knees started to weaken and Richard Bruton, who had called Enda 'wooden' in a *Hot Press* interview a few months hither, decided that Kenny wasn't so much leadership timber as MDF. Richard laid down his gauntlet, Enda Kenny sacked him, and it was officially on like Donkey Kong.

For a while, it looked as if Bruton and the 11 of the 19 frontbenchers who backed him would dispatch Kenny with ease. With the likes of Brian Hayes, Leo Varadkar, Simon Coveney, Joe McHugh, Lucinda Creighton and the general thrust of the young tigers and urban wing of the party, Bruton appeared to hold all the cards. It looked especially likely when Enda Kenny's positively *avant-garde* choice to step in at Finance, Kieran O'Donnell, defected to Camp Bruton after about 48 hours.

Losing supporters and lacking multiple dimensions, and with the majority of the Reservoir Pups on the other side, Enda Kenny looked spent. But then two important things happened.

First, Enda Kenny is the Charlton Heston of Irish politics: he'd waited patiently for 27 years to take the helm, and with power so close you'd have to grasp leadership from his cold, dead hands. So he and his backers in the country and western wing of the party fought like Trojans to make the grassroots feel loved/vaguely fearful of recrimination. The big factor in this whip round was Big Phil Hogan, thus setting in motion the strongman image he'd bulldoze into government (see *The Time Phil Hogan Charged Us to Deal with Our Shite*).

Second, Camp Bruton, which either through naiveté, lack of bottle or good old-fashioned complacency, ran the worst political coup since Guy Fawkes. Except if Richard Bruton and his cohort had been down by the Houses of Parliament that 5th of November, they would have stocked the basement with crates of mayonnaise.

When the time to vote confidence in Kenny came, it proved to be The Night of the Long Butter Knives: Kenny gave a speech that won a standing ovation, and won by a margin we'll apparently never know, as all the ballots had been shredded. The likes of Kieran O'Donnell no doubt empathise.

When Kenny came to reshuffle his front bench, he was relatively magnanimous. The Patrick Bateman wing of the party was well represented in Varadkar, Creighton and Coveney, although Hayes was out. Richard Bruton, too talented to be left out in spite, literally ran to stand still having been shifted to Enterprise, which he administered in government thirteen years earlier.

Meanwhile, Kenny's trustiest lieutenants, Reilly, Shatter, Hogan and Kehoe, had their place in Fine Gael high command galvanised. And Kieran O'Donnell's vacation of the Finance brief left room for his constituency and party colleague Michael Noonan to return to the front. As with Cosgrave and John Bruton before him, Enda would be in office within a year after the failed coup.

We'll never know of course how different it all could have been. What if Richard Bruton had won the leadership decisively, and with personal approval ratings hitting the ozone layer, then won the election decisively too? What if he'd won an overall majority and was able to govern alone? What if he'd just kept his powder dry and became Minister for Finance, would he have fared any better than Noonan? What if the split had been much more protracted and bitter, could Eamon Gilmore have ended up Taoiseach? Ah no, that's too far.

❖

Perpetual Embarrassment Rating: 7/10
Every time Enda has his picture taken in an embarrassing press shoot, Richard Bruton must think, 'That could have been me.'

National Peril-o-meter: 3/10
Opposition parties committing serial regicide is a key part of democracy. Of course, most times it works.

'Ah, lads!' Rating: 9/10
It should have been a slam dunk, but apparently Fine Gael men can't jump.

Length of time before Leo Varadkar gives it another try himself:
I'm surprised he hasn't done it already.

The Time Mick Wallace
Was Mick Wallace

During the Great Dáil Spring Clean of 2011, you got the impression that some of the people elected under those circumstances wouldn't have been at the races electorally in more salubrious times, a time when at the races was the most likely place to find your local TD. Mick Wallace was one such person.

Wallace is an intriguing character: a man who studied Arts in UCD but found himself in construction, a property developer who helped out a communist bookshop with digs, a man who raked it in during the Celtic Tiger but never lost his look of a man who harpoons fish for sustenance. Sherlock Holmes would struggle to figure out this Study in Pink.

Ah, the pink. Someone once gave him the advice of 'get a suit, get a haircut, get involved in Fianna Fáil' when he started making it big but Mick never paid a blind bit of heed, instead choosing to indulge his loud and proud

love of pink shirts. Like, deliberately pink, not just the result of a whitewash gone wrong. His love of the pink stems from his even more vibrant love of Italy (hence his brainchild, Dublin's Italian quarter) and particularly Italian football (hence his company, Wallace Calcio Ltd). He's a hardcore Juventus fan, a team that in their early days wore, you guessed it, pink and black. They're also the same colours, incidentally, as his beloved Wexford Youths League of Ireland team.

It was this sportsman's mix of unbridled passion, propensity for off-the-ball incidents and 1980s Italian league striker appearance (the Claudio Can-eejit look, if you will) that would lead to Mick's constant, ahem, Serie A unfortunate events.

For starters, he and his sartorial brothers in scruff justice, the Oscar the Grouch T-shirt-wearing Ming Flanagan and the oft-flannelled Richard Boyd Barrett, raised the ire of the traditionalists, whose monocles popped out at the state of these unruly backbenchers. A failed charge to impose a dress code was led by Michelle Mulherin (sure who else?).

Maybe if Mary Mitchell O'Connor had worn some trackies and a pair of Asics into the Dáil she might not have attracted the attention she did from Mick Wallace, who notoriously called her Miss Piggy on an open mic. He commented that she had 'toned down' what his backbench neighbour Shane Ross agreed were her 'garish colours', which was the most laughable example of a pot–kettle interface in recent history.

He gave a genuinely contrite apology, though, saying, 'It's hard to defend the indefensible. I'm completely out of order. I haven't a leg to stand on.'

He was similarly bang to rights when he gave an interview to RTÉ inexplicably volunteering the anecdote that he once involved a hit man in sorting out a debt. In fairness to him, he originally told the story to *Business & Finance* magazine in 2005, but now he was a TD it developed a more unsettling dimension. Wallace explained he was being messed around to the tune of €20,000 by a builder. So he, to quote his quite nifty euphemistic phrasing, 'knew of a guy who made a living out of a gun' (which makes it sound like he whittles pistols out of wood in a log cabin somewhere) and used him as 'leverage' to sabre-rattle the miscreant builder into coughing up. What seemed like a funny anecdote in 2005 didn't have anyone laughing in 2012.

It was particularly unfunny given just how unkempt his own financial affairs had become. In October 2011 he turned his pockets inside out and had butterflies fly out when the Commercial Court asked him to repay ACC Bank the €20 million he owed them. In June 2012 it emerged he settled a €2 million sum with the Revenue over under-declared VAT returns, and also doubled the wages he and his son took from the now insolvent company in 2008. In a fantastic demonstration of the circle of political life, he pledged to pay back his debt to the State by siphoning off half of his Dáil salary to pay for it. Not exactly robbing Peter to pay Peter, but something pretty close. In the face of several TDs suggesting Mick takes his pink slip, he responded in classic fashion – by heading off to the football in Poland for Euro 2012.

All this caused very traditional ructions among the

New Age backbenchers. 'Smirking tax cheat Wallace "has no respect" for peers' was the gloomy analysis of relations within the Dáil Technical Group by the *Irish Independent*. Joe Higgins and Mick argued about who was told what and when about the state of his financial affairs, and Clare Daly arguably cut him more slack than she would have had he got that haircut and joined Fianna Fáil.

His relationship with Clare Daly was all over the media at the time too. He insisted they were just good friends, but the papers, like an elderly aunt seeing you with a member of the opposite sex and asking, 'Is this the new one?', gleefully reported them dining out and pictured them walking together.

Among the chief tongue-waggers was (sure who else?) Eoghan Harris, who in paying her a compliment somehow managed to sort-of pay one to himself as well, describing Deputy Daly as '… a very attractive woman, especially to men who have moved beyond the blonde bimbo stage … if she were conventionally pretty it would diminish her power to make men of the world pay attention.'

OK then.

Clare's resolution to stand by Mick caused consternation on the left and when she resigned from the Socialist Party they went as far as to say she valued her relationship with him over her relationship with the party, but hey, at least the worst of his hit-man-hiring, VAT-neglecting capers were over, right? I mean, it's not like he would become embroiled in a ruckus with the gardai and Minister for Justice over his driving habits and the way the aforementioned dealt with that information, right? Oh …

❖

Perpetual Embarrassment Rating: 7/10
The presence of Animal from *The Muppets* in the Dáil always causes a double take, in fairness.

National Peril-o-meter: 6/10
His debts are a drop in the ocean, really.

'Ah, lads!' Rating: 8/10
A builder gets a hitman to settle a debt … wasn't Colin Farrell in that film?

Still feel a bit queasy over that Harris quote about Clare Daly?
Yeah, me too.

The Time Holy Joes Lost
the Head over Natural Highs

Ireland has long had a complex issue with substance abuse. The nation's collective love of the drop (see *The Time Limerick Was Allowed to Drink But Nobody Else Was*) is the basis of many's an international punch line, with drink and Irish people going together like koalas and eucalyptus, or zombie koalas and brains. Yet this is also the country of the Pioneer temperance movement. It's also home to a dedicated cohort of cognitively dissonant, morally panicked busybodies.

Having been going discreetly for some time, head shops suddenly became Exhibit A in the case against social and moral decay. With one said to be opening in Ireland every week in January 2010, their unique selling point was 'natural highs', herbal, synthetic and most crucially legal alternatives to marijuana, cocaine and what not.

One student speaking to the *University Observer* said,

'I wouldn't buy stuff every week, but it's good to stock up every now and again.'

So with this new phenomenon of students going for the big shop in these head shops popping up like mushrooms (the magic variety of which were banned in 2006, incidentally), it fell to the Seanad to attempt to understand, with a balanced, nuanced debate on the matter. Uh oh.

Hip to the groove Senator Ronan Mullen was predictably open-minded: 'We should consider banning not merely the drugs sold but also head shops ... One need only consider the paraphernalia and products sold and promoted, whether on T-shirts or through other merchandise, to see how profoundly antisocial these establishments are. Parents and teachers are right to be outraged about the phenomenon that is head shops.'

These kids, with their legal drugs, and T-shirts with words on them! Topping that though was Fianna Fáil Senator Geraldine Feeney, who offered a litany of gems better than Al Pacino's speech in *Any Given Sunday*:

'When I was researching this subject, I became a little bit of an expert. I am now very familiar with words such as "Snow Blow", "Nirvana" and "Stone Zone", which the Cathaoirleach will not know ... One does not have to be too bright to know these are a gateway to harder drugs. The products are deliberately aimed at the young population, which is worrying.'

Impressively managing not to suffocate under her own self-righteous smuggery, she continued: 'Our hands are tied because technically the shops have the right to exist, yet they have no right to exist in the minds of God-fearing, good-living people.'

Carrying on down the non-prejudicial, non-presumptuous route, she added: 'The people I see hanging around head shops – I am not out too late at night – are young teenagers under 18. Perhaps they are not sold the goods when they go into the shops but they probably have somebody buying them for them.'

Brilliant. Mary Harney, the then Health Minister, praised Feeney's tour de force as well as the other inputs to the debate: 'A sensible approach has been taken by all Members.'

Only one notable political representative eschewed the pat-on-the-back fest, notorious renegade and MD Jim McDaid. He said it would be a 'huge mistake' to close head shops, as 'If we ban those drugs we are going to lose control of these drugs to the street people again.'

The prohibitive zeal was very much present in his back yard of Letterkenny, though, as a crowd of 300 protested against a head shop there. Their leader, Tom Conaghan of the Anti-Head Shops Committee, kept the alarmist tenor when he said, 'Today we marched behind the Ardaghey Band, will we be marching behind a hearse the next time?'

Hearses were very nearly needed not long after, as a pipe bomb was discovered outside Letterkenny's Yutopia head shop. RAAD (that's Republican Action Against Drugs – in case you were thinking they were surfer dudes or something) claimed responsibility for what they called 'their first and only warning'. Within a few days, the shop was closed. Local anti-drugs campaigner P.J. Blake called for a garda special unit, as 'There is a very serious rise in the amount of robberies and theft and a disturbing increase in the amount of violence. We have had bombings and a fire here.' This was the only reference he made to the reason the head shop closed.

It was a similar story all over the country, as some of the more extreme opponents to head shops booming thought that the answer would be a head shop bombing. In Sligo a head shop and sex shop was damaged in a fire (killing two moral menaces with one stone, I suppose). A similar sex and drugs set-up (which one local claimed was getting 'a rowdy element') was destroyed in similar circumstances in Dublin's Capel Street. Two viable devices were found outside a head shop in Athlone, while a petrol bomb was also found outside a Dundalk head shop. The culprits were thought to be miffed drug dealers, making it perhaps the only time pushers, paramilitaries and pious campaigners were on the same side of an argument.

The Dundalk petrol bomb proved to be the last straw for Louth TD and Justice Minister Dermot Ahern, who along with Mary Harney introduced legislation to restrict what could be sold in head shops. The laws were on the books by August, meaning that from proliferation to legislation took less than nine months, the quickest the Irish government has moved on anything for quite some time.

Fianna Fáil TD Chris Andrews, talking favourably about banning head shops, said, 'I have been greatly concerned by the recent reports detailing the potential serious health risks associated with the consumption of many of the products available in these retail outlets.'

The year after the head shop hysteria, a study was published that 672 people died due to alcohol poisoning in the four years between 2004 and 2008, with 3,336 deaths due to alcohol dependence. But at least we got rid of the Snow Blow, right?

❖

Perpetual Embarrassment Rating: 8/10
Geraldine Feeney should have her own daytime talk show. It would be a YouTube sensation.

National Peril-o-meter: 8/10
Dammit, man, don't you see our children are under mortal danger from Triple Sod, Clarkie Cat and Yellow Bentines?!

'Ah, lads!' Rating: 10/10
Remember, kids, follow the example of responsible, moral adults and just burn things you disagree with.

Number of pubs passed on anti-head shop vigil routes:
Loads.

The Time the Government Nearly Made Itself Illegal

No story better sums up the surreal nature of Irish politics than the recurring cheese nightmare that was Brian Cowen's last few days and weeks in office.

The dislodged bumper of Cowen's clapped-out banger of state was already causing sparks on the road. It emerged at the start of January 2011 that mere weeks before the bank guarantee that made sure nothing was ever certain again, Cowen and Seanie Fitzpatrick had a 'social' game of golf together at Druid's Glen. They apparently avoided discussing bank business like the tricky sand trap on the 13th, although how they were able to play at all with such a large elephant in the way is beyond me.

Following the revelations, it seemed likely that the Fianna Fáil parliamentary party had the requisite votes to table a motion of no confidence in the leader, but at this point the members seemed to lose confidence in themselves, giving

Brian Cowen a chance to give the rebels the puppy dog eyes treatment individually over the weekend, rather than as a baying mob like they originally hoped. Before any malcontent could put up a no-confidence motion, Cowen placed a motion of confidence in himself, at which point everyone outside the party got motion sickness.

Of all the heavy hitters who were out for Cowen, only Micheál Martin put his arse on the line for the hiding to nothing. He lost the ensuing leadership vote in an oddly sanguine contest that bore closer resemblance to friends arguing over a lunch bill, a stark difference from the days when Fianna Fáil leadership heaves actually killed people. But embarrassing though his defeat was, he still came out of it better than the gun-shy Brian Lenihan, and Mary Hanafin. Hanafin looked particularly daft, as weeks of nods and winks about her future intentions turned out to be nothing but a nervous twitch.

While interviewed on the news about her reticence, she claimed she voted against Cowen remaining party leader, but still had confidence in him as Taoiseach, a phrase which if deciphered should probably earn you a million pound prize. Lenihan, meanwhile, told the press he was backing Cowen, but was immediately contradicted by backbencher John McGuinness, who swore blind Lenihan was planning some kind of *Ocean's Eleven*-style heist on the big chair. But while Lenihan and Hanafin hoisted themselves by their own petards, it was Martin who fell on his sword and resigned forthwith. And that's when the fun started.

As it turned out, Micheál resigning was the first domino to fall that would eventually bring down the whole house of cards, as he had no Monopoly in resigning during a political Twister of catastrophic and even Ludocrous proportions. No sooner had Martin stepped down than Mary Harney finally relinquished her kung fu grip on the Department of Health after deciding she wasn't going to run in the next election. She was soon followed by Tony Killeen at Defence, who cited health reasons for stepping down, and Noel Dempsey and Dermot Ahern, who stepped down for defence reasons. The Statler & Waldorf of cabinet, who resigned after their 'Bailout, what bailout?' press conference a few weeks previously, would have struggled to get the number one preferences of anyone who wasn't a cousin or closer, so they probably did right. And then there were ten.

Bullish after facing down his detractors, and having just created five new public sector jobs, Brian Cowen saw an opportunity to refresh his front bench for the election and put the last fortnight's grizzly business behind him by appointing some new ministers. But like hot coffee placed on a dashboard, things got burned and messy fast.

The public bristled at the idea from the get go, who saw it as the political equivalent of spritzing aftershave when what's really needed is a powerhose. They didn't much like the idea of a swathe of new TDs getting ministerial pensions for the 45 minutes they'd be in situ either. The Greens, who had responded to the Seanie Fitz news by saying they 'weren't Sherlock Holmes' (which should have been apparent after they banned deer stalking), in government hadn't been terribly successful in getting the government to do things they liked, but in this instance they were dead set on making sure the government didn't do something they didn't like. The plan was vetoed by Green Party leader John Gormley, who was backing away slowly to the door anyway. To add insult to injury, Cowen loyalist and Enterprise Minister Batt O'Keeffe resigned on the morning of the reshuffle. And then there were nine.

With Cowen's cabinet dropping like the last half hour of *The Departed*, and with no facility to inject fresh blood, Cowen proceeded to stack department upon department, creating cartoonishly large Uber-Ministries. Mary Hanafin, with a title that would flummox even the most skilled plaque engraver, became Minister for Tourism, Culture, Sport, Enterprise, Trade and Innovation. Meanwhile, Brendan Smith had responsibility for the hilariously diffuse portfolios of Justice and Agriculture. Alas, he never implemented the most logical policy of those dual roles: Farm Courts.

To make a bad situation worse, a few days later the Green Party's zen-like patience finally ran out and they withdrew from government, which had two big effects. First, it reduced the cabinet to its constitutional minimum of seven, meaning the government of the nation was one bad dose of man flu away from being completely illegal. And second, it meant that Social Protection, Defence,

Community, Rural & Gaeltacht Affairs, Environment, Heritage and Local Government, Communications, Energy and Natural Resources was the responsibility of just two lads.

Thankfully for Pat Carey and Éamon Ó Cuív, they weren't too heavily taxed as the Dáil was dissolved after a few days, thus ending our weeks-long national headache. Brian Cowen resigned as Fianna Fáil leader, but kept hold of the keys to Leinster House until a suitable replacement could be chosen by the people. Or failing someone suitable, someone who could get 15 people to the table at very least.

❖

Perpetual Embarrassment Rating: 10/10
Having to give up government due to a lack of attendance is pretty desperate.

National Peril-o-meter: 10/10
Literally as bad as it gets. Is there a Constitutional lawyer in the house?

Ah, lads! Rating: 9/10
Having ministers chopping and changing across Dublin offices must have been like something out of *Mrs Doubtfire*.

The difference between golfing and government?
Better you don't have a cabinet off scratch.

The Time Brian Lenihan Sr Looked Directly Down the Camera

'No one can beat Brian to the park' was the consensus in early 1990 with respect to Brian Lenihan's presidential election chances. With his affable demeanour and 'clown prince of politics' reputation, he was a dictionary definition of a sure thing. All he had to do was not lie about anything. What could possibly go wrong?

At one point Lenihan had an unassailable lead in the polls at 49 per cent, meaning he'd exceed the quota on the second count by sticking his tongue out. Those polling numbers changed thanks to another number: 1982.

Ah yes, 1982, the beginning of anno Domini in Irish political lunacy. Except instead of AD, we mark it 'GUBU'. Among the many, many ludicrous things done that year was an attempt at creating a constitutional calamity so terrible, if Charles Haughey had a DeLorean he would have destroyed the fabric of time and space. With Garret FitzGerald having lost supply thanks to the now notorious 'VAT on children's shoes' budget, Haughey wanted President Hillery to forbear in using one of the few weapons in the Áras' arsenal: refusing to dissolve a government. Reason being, if Hillery refused, Garrett would have to resign as Taoiseach, leaving Charlie free to try and form a government without the stress or cost of consulting the public.

To that end, Haughey, Clare TD Sylvester Barrett and, yes, Brian Lenihan called up their old buddy Paddy Hillery for a bit of a catch-up and oh, by the way, would you mind us being wildly disrespectful of constitutional procedure for a minute to help us out? Hillery told them where to go.

And then, as is often the case with an issue in Irish politics, nothing happened for eight years.

It was on a *Questions & Answers* episode prior to the election that Garret FitzGerald brought up the matter of phoning the President, and after that the good doctor walked away whistling while the machine overheated. Lenihan swore blind he never called the President to as much as say 'D'ya know who's dead?', but then along came a student called Jim Duffy. He was doing a postgrad thesis in UCD's Politics Department about the presidency, Lenihan was one of the interviewees and in May 1990 Duffy's college work became the biggest story in the country. As if students at the time who were approaching exams and procrastinating furiously didn't feel rotten enough.

Duffy let the tapes of his interview with Lenihan go public, and to say they were incriminating would be like saying the seventh circle of hell was a bit sticky. Phrases like 'Oh yeah, I mean I got through to him. I remember talking to him and he wanted us to lay off', for example, didn't sit very well with his record of events, or indeed sit well with anyone. Saying Hillery 'was annoyed with the whole bloody lot of us' and 'Looking back, it was a mistake on our part' didn't exactly help things.

With Lenihan's testimony all over the shop, he made the ill-fated decision to go on the RTÉ News with Sean 'Diggy' Duignan to try and explain himself out of trouble. Not only did he dig a hole for himself several storeys deep, he also added to Ireland's political lexicon: 'My mature recollection at this stage is I did not ring ...'

As audiences still tried to get their head around 'mature recollection', Lenihan, with fist clenched, turned to them as he finished the word 'ring', and, staring right down the camera, finished his sentence. '... President Hillery, and I want to put my reputation on the line in that respect.'

Oh boy.

When Duignan put it to him that either he was not telling the truth now or he wasn't telling the truth on the tapes to Duffy, he claimed he 'must have been mistaken' talking to Duffy, before adding, 'My mind was not attuned. I often oblige students in matters of this kind.'

But if suggesting he regularly agreed to talk to students and then just made things up like he's Abe Simpson was bad enough, on the tape he showed a bit more self-editing than the 'easy talk' he was insisting it was. 'We'll have to improve the phraseology of that,' he said over the reference to Haughey being 'gung ho'.

Oops.

Lenihan was walking wounded by this point. A poll showed only 18 per cent believed he was telling the truth, whatever it was. All of a sudden Mary Robinson was looking like a contender.

Worse still for Lenihan, not only did the job he was applying for look increasingly out of reach but the job he actually had was in jeopardy. Alan Dukes, obviously influenced by the Bill & Ted movies of the time, called Lenihan's position 'totally incredible and totally untenable'. The Opposition put down a motion of no confidence. Charles Haughey insisted his 'friend of 30 years' was going nowhere. The Progressive Democrats threatened to pull out of government if he didn't go and throw him out of power. Charles Haughey sacked him. Cos that's how he rolls.

Despite being thrown out of cabinet and being badly burned by Haughey, the expert renovators of the Fianna Fáil machine came out in force. He was buoyed by campaign rallies run with the slogan 'SIMPLY THE BEST', which I assume was a reference designed to win back supporters of Tina Turner and the *RTÉ Guide*.

All of a sudden, Lenihan was a Simba-esque character returning from adversity to make an honourable comeback. At least he was until Scar came along and ruined it. Pee Flynn simultaneously amplified his voice and muffled his brain by having a go at Mary Robinson's 'new-found interest in her family'.

Inevitably, there were ructions. 'I needed that like a hole in the head,' lamented Lenihan. For a man who had dug so many holes over the previous weeks, he knew what he was on about.

In the end Lenihan won a plurality of votes, 44 per cent of them, but it wasn't enough as Mary Robinson stormed through on the second count. Lenihan and Fianna Fáil tried to console themselves with the notion that they lost due to an anti-Fianna Fáil gang-up, but 56 per cent of the voting public knew otherwise. And so Mary Robinson, with her left-wing media buddies like Niall Tóibín, Mick Lally and Zig & Zag, became the first non-Fianna Fáil-endorsed President in the history of the State.

❖

Perpetual Embarrassment Rating: 9/10

'Brian, don't look down the camera, you're going to make an eejit of yourself. No, turn back to Diggy, Brian! BRIAN! NOOOO!'

National Peril-o-meter: 9/10

If President Hillery hadn't been quite so sure of himself or had allowed Haughey to bully him, the Constitution would have blown up in everyone's face.

'Ah, lads!' Rating: 8/10

I still want to know more about his habit of talking to students without attuning his mind.

Poor Austin Currie doesn't get much of a mention here, does he?

Yeah, he's a bit like Christopher Lee in the last *Lord of the Rings* film.

The Time Eamon Gilmore Showed Jerry Maguire the Certificate of Irishness

Be it a school prize-giving, a ten-week computer course, or a volunteering weekend, nothing quite says 'achievement' like getting a certificate. And if you get it framed, as opposed to say keeping it from crinkling by putting it in a large book or something, then you're really cooking with gas.

It was this line of logic that must have been used when the Department of Foreign Affairs resolved to give Tom Cruise a gift in April 2013 for having Irish relatives. Because, sure why not? But once you resolve to give Tom Cruise a present, what do you actually get a man as well resourced as he is? €20 in a card? Probably won't go very far with him. Disconcertingly intense eyes? Nah, he already has a bunch of those. A voucher for flying lessons? Oh, right …

And then, I like to imagine some diplomat mandarin up around Saint Stephen's Green had a light bulb moment: 'Here, how about … giving him a certificate with a nice frame?'

'A certificate, brilliant! Someone get that man a medal!'

As Minister for Foreign Affairs, it fell to Eamon Gilmore to officiate at this ceremony, and he was probably just glad to get something to do. After all, since coming to office in 2011 Labour under his leadership hasn't done much more than grimace across the table from their partners in office and see Labour's stock fall like pumpkin sales in November.

So with it looking likelier that Eamon and his memory-foam mattress ministers would be relieved of the pressure of reading the national roadmap of change (especially since differentiating between his way and Frankfurt's way has proven quite a challenge), small wonder he was up for a bit of glamour.

As it turns out, Tom Cruise's family is sort of a big deal. He can trace his family back (and can do it with ease now that Tourism Ireland did it for him) down the line to Richard FitzGilbert 'Strongbow' de Clare, and among his more recent ancestors was Patrick Russell Cruise, a Famine-era landlord who reinstated evicted tenants from their homes. And somewhere in between, a bunch of his family stuck it to Cromwell too.

Tom Cruise, born Thomas Cruise Mapothor (is

he anything to the Ballyvaughan Mapothors?), was characteristically enthusiastic about his 'awesome heritage' and said he was incredibly proud to be Irish (he was hardly going to say, 'No, I'm bored off my arse and wish I was Norwegian', now was he?) but he also said that his Irish pride was pivotal in him making *Far and Away*. He said this with a straight face, which is a great tribute to his self-discipline and acting skill.

And so with a knight, a rebel and a Famine landlord in the family, it's surely only a matter of time before Tom does an Irish *Braveheart*. Eamon may already be masterminding the logistics to get a bit of foreign investment into the country, but the film Tom Cruise was in Dublin to promote in the first place doesn't augur well omens-wise for Eamon: *Oblivion*.

❖

Perpetual Embarrassment Rating: 4/10
Eamon isn't exactly a red carpet sort of guy, but he didn't do too badly compared to, say, John Bruton (see *The Time John Bruton Laid It on with a Shovel for Prince Charles*).

National Peril-o-meter: 3/10
Any potential danger to the State has to be a lot less likely now we have Ethan Hunt onside.

'Ah, lads!' Rating: 7/10

A certificate of Irishness seemed a bit sparse … what about an emerald hurley?

Chances of Brendan Gleeson or Colm Meaney being in any potential Cruise film set in Ireland:

It'll be a statutory requirement, surely?

The Time Brendan Smith Offered Everyone a Whole Pile of Cheese

The West Wing's lovably crotchety Chief of Staff Leo McGarry would throughout the series tell the story of President Andrew Jackson, who in the main foyer of the White House had a two-ton block of cheese. It was there for the hungry, or people who were just into big lumps of cheese. But either way, it was available to the public and a compelling symbol of public access to the President. Or, at least, his cheese.

At Christmas 2010, former Agriculture Minister Brendan Smith took Leo rather too literally.

The day before Smith went on *Morning Ireland* to publicise a new government initiative, €6 billion in cuts and tax raises had been announced. In both real and morale terms, it was an incredibly dark time. But fear not, as Smith gleefully announced on the biggest news show in the country that 167 tonnes of EU cheese (over 83 times as much as Andrew Jackson had at his White

WHY IRISH WELFARE RECIPIENTS APPEAR to be HAPPY WELFARE RECIPIENTS...

CHEESE!

House) would be distributed to needy causes. 'Cheese would be made available,' he announced, to those 'who are living in poor circumstances and are under pressure.'

Calamity ensued.

Even though the initiative had been around for ages, it used to be in butter form, before mixing it up for 2010 as, 'Cheese is easier to distribute than butter.' Delivery-wise, that is. Not on toast, like.

Agriculture spokesman for Fine Gael Andrew Doyle was quick off the mark with an eye-catching comparison: 'This government is behaving like Marie Antoinette did. Yesterday they announce cuts of €6 billion that are going to be imposed on the public, and today they're as good as saying "Let them eat cheese".' In fairness to Marie, at least she offered a bit of bread to go with it.

The announcement itself, coupled with the wildly off-kilter timing, meant that the public's reaction was swift and angry. On Ireland's home of swift anger, RTÉ's *Liveline*, came comments like: 'It's an appalling insult to the poor,' 'They're throwing muck in our faces [there's an idea, free spa days for the poor?], Marie Antoinette saying "Let them eat cake" was the start of the revolution, is that what they want?' and 'It's a disgrace, Joe, I've been sittin' in traffic for over an hour, Joe! The council are a disgrace, Joe!', although that last comment may have been made later in the programme.

John Monaghan of Saint Vincent de Paul noted that loads of money was available for the banks but only cheese was available for the poor. But, with the Curate's Egg optimism you only get in organisations like that, added that anything that would contribute to solid meals for people would be appreciated, and asked the minister for any other food he could get his hands on too.

Minister Smith, not expecting to be torn to pieces and thrown in a fondue pot, seemed personally wounded by the whole thing. He wouldn't have liked the reaction of the international press in which case then, as the *Guardian*, *Independent* and *Daily Mail* picked it up and the Mail running with the headline 'Irish government become laughing stock'. Though I suppose it was generous of them to suggest we weren't a laughing stock before. The public at large were just as cutting, but a lot funnier.

Online and in the newspapers, the puns piled up as plentifully as the cheese mountain. 'Un-brie-lievable', 'I camembert this country anymore' and 'You gouda be kidding me' among the best. When Brendan Smith looks back at his ministerial career, he'll probably look back at his *Morning Ireland* cheese mobilisation announcement and realise that as his days in office went, he'd had grater.

❖

Perpetual Embarrassment Rating: 9/10

Did he not think before he went on *Morning Ireland*, 'Hold on, what chance is there I'll become The Cheese Guy for the rest of my life?' Though maybe that boosted Smith's (manch)ego.

National Peril-o-meter: 8/10

If revolution had actually broken out, the Dáil getting cheesed would have been pretty damaging. Possibly on a par(mesan) with the French Revolution.

'Ah, lads!' Rating: 10/10

Any government that reckons they can follow up swingeing cuts with an announcement about alleviating cheese measures has truly gone (em)mental.

Are you done with the cheese puns?

Paneer-ly ... now I'm done.

The Time Ray Burke
Pulled Up Trees out of Spite

It was the beginning of the 1980s, a decade that belonged to venal, ambitious go-getters. And Charles Haughey was as venal, ambitious and go-getting as they got.

You could fill an entire book with the mad, bad and dangerous stuff Haughey got up to. In fact, quite a few people have. Joe Joyce and Peter Murtagh's *The Boss* is the definitive book profiling the genuinely traumatic circumstances of his 1982 government, when GUBU became a four-letter word. *The Boss* was voted by Irish politicians as the best ever book about politics in a 1996 survey, beating, fittingly enough, Machiavelli's *The Prince*.

Stephen Collins' *The Power Game* is similarly brilliant, reading like a thriller until you shake yourself and remember that it's not fiction. But in it are some terrific anecdotes, like the legend of Haughey chasing after a woman, completely starkers, down a field of a house where a party was being thrown attended by Grace Kelly. Or the fact that for every eight quid AIB had on their books at one point in the 1970s, Charlie had one of them. Or when they eventually moved to take his chequebook away he replied with the line, 'I need that to live!' But within those supposedly frivolous stories a great truth is revealed: Haughey saw himself as a Renaissance prince, but in reality he ran the country like an *enfant terrible*.

Think about it: the running around in the nip, the cavalier attitude to money, the ability to turn from angelic to temperamental brat in 0.4 seconds. It all adds up. Add to that his love of gifts and gadgets like horsies, helicopters and private islands, and the fact he once nicked bugging equipment from a senior guard, who in turn had it lent to him by the RUC, and it starts to get a bit eerie. The only seven-year-old boy cliché he didn't seem to have was an interest in dinosaurs.

He even had his own incredibly well-kitted-out treehouse up in Kinsealy, to complement his Batcave-cum-Tracy Island down in Inishvickillaun. And it was with his north Dublin partner in juvenile hell-raising, Ray 'Rambo' Burke, that they created one of their more ludicrous capers.

It's well worth remembering that as well as being a full-time mod con collector, Charles Haughey was, a fair bit of the time, also a politician. Specifically, he was an incredibly trigger-happy politician when it came to hot-button electoral decisions, and had a lousy shot to boot. After assuming leadership of Fianna Fáil in 1979 following a decade in the long grass, Haughey's love of the fight and the roll of the dice seemed to trump the need for stability. He called an election in 1981 when he had no real need to and lost serious ground, and as a result had to endure another two in the next 18 months. Of those three elections, he lost two.

But the one he didn't lose, in February 1982, led, as we already mentioned, to one of the most chaotic and insane terms of office the world has ever seen. But apart from giving the world the phrase GUBU, it also gave Clonsilla in west Dublin some trees. Which were taken away soon after.

With Haughey holding together a government majority with masking tape and glue, he came up with an ingenious plan to solidify his majority. There was just one problem: it was rubbish.

Brussels was in the market for an Irish EC Commissioner at the time and Haughey resolved to appoint former Commissioner Dick Burke, even though he was an Opposition TD and former Fine Gael minister. But far from being a show of magnanimity, Haughey reckoned Burke's seat in Dublin West was winnable in a by-election. When he was accused of gamesmanship he suggested the charge was a low blow. Garret FitzGerald called his bluff and asked, if he was genuine then, not to put a Fianna Fáil candidate up. Haughey started whistling and backing away towards the door.

He of course did run a candidate, and to mitigate the monster risk he was taking made it a big hitter: Eileen Lemass. She was a former TD herself who had only been recently unseated and, like her party leader Haughey, had married into one of the most significant families in Irish politics. She was up against Fine Gael's Liam Skelly, a newcomer to the political scene but a local businessman and he was pushed hard as a solid community candidate.

The relative political experience of the two was quite diverse, but just to be sure, Fianna Fáil's pre-eminent hard case of the time, Rambo Burke, was to be the Director of Elections. Presumably while having a campaign strategy brainstorm one morning, he had a eureka moment and went, 'Trees! We'll plant some trees! Punters bloody love foliage!' And so plant some trees he did, but just for the good of it, mind, and if there happened there were a few newspapermen with cameras there too, sure wouldn't it be a bonus?

On election day, the combination of a big bruiser of a campaign manager, a candidate with top-drawer name recognition and that unmistakable new tree smell was thought to be enough to take the seat, and thus solidify their working majority. Which, if you'll remember, was the whole point of this needlessly complex stroke. But it wasn't enough. After the first count Lemass was ahead, but only by 300 votes, but after transfers Skelly came out on top. Haughey's plan backfired, and Rambo went Hulk, removing the trees with 'feck ye all' glee and taking us all for saps. Burke would, of course, become for Irish political corruption what Athens is for the Olympics.

It was incredible cynicism, but just a regular day at the frequently picketed office back in the eighties. Not for the first time and certainly not for the last time, Haughey bet massive on a half-chance and was near blown off the edge. But for Haughey, the edge was where he did his best work.

❖

Perpetual Embarrassment Rating: 1/10
Burke's shame is so low it's swimming round his ankles.

National Peril-o-meter: 7/10
Someone could break their neck in those tree holes!

'Ah, lads!' Rating: 9/10
Risking your party voice in Europe to try and gain an extra seat. What were they thinking?

What did he do with the trees?
Kinsealy would have been a decent home for them.

The Time Willie O'Dea Pulled Out His Strap and Laid Some Busters Down

In a political scene that takes its cultural cues more from showbands, Willie O'Dea is about as close as we get to gangsta rap. He represents Limerick city, which I suppose in a sense is the Irish equivalent of being Straight Outta Compton. He furiously pounds the pavements, carefully curating his voters with his enormous posse, so he's still got love for the streets. He was against Haughey for most of the eighties during the various internecine Fianna Fáil heaves, a dispute which in its own way made the Biggy and Tupac feud look pretty tame.

After years being dissed by the leadership, in 2004 he finally got a cabinet berth and ministerial Merc, a G car if ever there was one. It was his shot at the big time, but it was a picture of him looking like he was about to take a shot that nearly caused him to blow it.

Unfortunately for the never publicity-shy O'Dea, he didn't take Chuck D's famous advice: don't believe the hype. But being Minister for Defence down The Curragh with all those soldiers and guns does mad things for the testosterone balance. And when you add in his love for getting his name in the paper, Notorious Wee O'Dea's blood rushed to his head. And his trigger finger.

Some poor enterprising soul of a photographer must have said, 'Here, Willie, give us an oul "pew pew pew!" pose there!' and, not to be shown up in front of the big, bad soldier men, in his best Nate Dogg pose pulled out his strap right down the camera. Hilarity ensues, with Joe Higgins and Pat Rabbitte in the Dáil having a go at Willie's attempt to pop a cap.

But the embarrassment of staring back at everyone who bought a newspaper while waving a piece around was nothing compared to what happened when Willie went back to street fighting, old-skool style. He tried to ice an opponent gaining on his turf, namely Sinn Féin's Maurice Quinlivan. How did he do it? He claimed Quinlivan's brother was a straight-up P-I-M-P. Or rather, a secret one, suggesting he was involved in the running of a brothel in the city. He later denied saying this and he even signed a sworn affidavit that he never said anything of the sort. And that's when the po-lice got involved.

The *Limerick Leader* published an interview with O'Dea in March 2009 in which he was quoted as saying, 'I suppose I'm going a bit too far when I say this but I'd like to ask Mr Quinlivan is the brothel still closed?'

You're right, Willie, you did go too far. The brothel remark referred to a house that Sinn Féin councillor Maurice Quinlivan's brother Nessan was renting out. He had no idea, when three women were arrested at that house for brothel-keeping, that it was going on there, as cat houses are a bit like Lotto winners: you know they exist, but you've never actually seen one. When Willie swore blind, and indeed an affidavit, that he didn't say anything of the kind, the journalist pulled out a strap of his own, his recorder. Unlike the one in The Curragh, this piece was loaded. Willie's defence – that he forgot he said all that stuff – somehow failed to cut any ice, as a barrister signing an affidavit of that nature is as stupid as putting a hose to his eye to see why water wasn't coming out.

Making an embarrassing retraction and the law up in his grill, he had to pay damages for his trash talking, but that wasn't enough. The haters were after him. A confidence motion was put down, which was defeated as the Green Party didn't vote against him. Well, not all the Green Party. Party chairman Dan Boyle didn't have a seat in the Dáil, but he did have a Twitter account, and used it to say that O'Dea should resign, and he was gone by the end of the week. No more regulating for Willie.

For people in Limerick, it was far from A Good Day as they regretted losing their minister, even if 63 per cent of people in the place thought he had to go, according to a *Limerick Leader* poll. Willie would later make an indignant *Late Late Show* appearance, railing on the punk Greens for blasting him, whom he seemed to view as a kind of Smeagol/Gollum-type character, first meek and pitiful, then pure evil. The audience cheered him on at every turn.

His website statement summed it up: 'Collective responsibility is rendered meaningless where Green parliamentarians can appear to be making sanctioned statements of Green party policy that run contrary to the position agreed at the cabinet table by their government colleagues.'

Indeed. I mean, God forbid someone would make an official statement at variance with the truth.

One benefit of the whole affair for Willie was an unexpected boost in his street cred, thanks to the talents of Limerick city's finest musical comics The Rubberbandits on YouTube. Released at the height of his troubles, the portrayal of Willie as a streetwise, hash-selling, falsetto singer who implores one of the Bandits to egg the Dáil rather took the sting out. He gained even more kudos a few months later when he went on *Liveline* and publicly defended The Rubberbandits, maintaining his sense of humour despite a barrage of 'That Horse Outside, Joe, is a disgrace, Joe! Are ya listenin', Joe? Joe? JOE?!'

O'Dea said, 'I think the reputation of Limerick would be damaged far, far more if we were put across as dour, humourless people who don't even have the capacity to laugh at ourselves.' Drawing reference to the band's previous, him-heavy video, he added, 'I was mercilessly lampooned and I didn't call in to *Liveline* to complain because what they did was funny and I can laugh at myself.'

To his credit, Willie might have had 99 problems, but a sketch ain't one.

❖

Perpetual Embarrassment Rating: 8/10
A grown man posing with a firearm is one thing, a lawyer swearing an incorrect affidavit is quite another.

National Peril-o-meter: 5/10
Negligible, but the photographer was probably bricking it for a while, though.

'Ah, lads!' Rating: 8/10
In retrospect, Willie probably accepts that the 'Intimate that a rival's brother is a massive hoormaster' method of political takedown was fraught with risk.

Moustache: 8/10
In fairness, it is eerily beautiful.

The Time Photoshopping Referendum Posters Became a Craze

The problem with referenda is that they're bloody awful. They boil complex and sometimes diffuse legal issues down to a binary and visceral response, often a million miles away from the question actually being asked. It's like trying to conduct surgery with a Fisher-Price screwdriver. But the Irish Constitution requires that we use My First Tool Kit before amending it.

This leads invariably to bitterly irrational division and shocking reductive debate that drifts away from the original point like a bearded man on a raft off a desert island swept up in a strong ocean current with only a stick man for company. Or, indeed, drifts away like the previous sentence.

But one of the upsides to such a setup is the inevitable descent into comic madness it facilitates, and posters and slogans are generally the conduit. At the time of the original divorce referendum in 1986, former dressmaker turned political battleaxe Alice Glenn came up with the gem that 'Women voting for divorce is like turkeys voting for Christmas.' That was but the headline though in a whole pamphlet outlining reasons not to let divorce pass, like the monetary cost to the government of setting up the framework to 'introduce a **DIVORCE CULTURE** [her capitalising and bolding, not mine] on our impoverished little nation'.

She also pleaded that 'Because of the tendency to summon emotionally charged arguments, it is necessary … to think clearly about the cold facts about divorce.' A few lines down the same paragraph, after making this sober call for a non-dramatic discussion of the issues, she said, 'Once the gates for divorce have been opened, the clamour for more and more divorce goes unabated. You may as well hold back the tides with your hands.'

In the nine years that passed between referenda, attitudes to divorce softened significantly, but the No side's histrionics were still very much alive. Billboards with the tagline 'Hello Divorce … Bye Bye Daddy … Vote NO!' loomed over the country, and even then the re-run referendum carried by 0.6 per cent. But, of course, in the following decade we'd become very acquainted with re-runs. The Lisbon Treaty referenda were heartbreakingly stupid, and the Death Star of crass postering.

The Yes side did what they normally did and assumed everyone was smart enough to agree with them, or rather not dumb enough to be against them. Hence posters with anodyne slogans like 'Yes for Jobs' and 'Keep Ireland at the Heart of Europe'. But while some had the faint hint of not trying, or had the sense that Ireland was a kind of geopolitical stent, that wasn't all the Yes side had to offer. The worst of all was Young Fine Gael's risible attempt at sexy humour. No, you read that right. One of the leaflets featured a J. Arthur Rank gong-basher-style human male torso (he appeared to have no head, and could you blame him?) sporting tight blue and yellow pants with the tagline 'Enlarge your opportunities'. Worse still was their female version (gender balance, yeah!) where a girl is holding actual bloody melons with the slogan 'Increase your prospects'. Actual bloody melons.

But while the Yes side sat back on its melons, sorry, laurels, the No side ran a tour de force of imaginative postering that framed the campaign. What a pity they were utterly shameless to boot.

The conservative pressure group Cóir did most of the running on this, running hot pink love hearts on lampposts with slogans like 'The EU **LOVES** Control' (again, their bold capitalising, not mine). But by far their most notorious posters were the ongoing series of Jamaican-coloured posters with alarming statements in, you guessed it, capitalised bold letters.

'**95% OF EUROPEANS WOULD VOTE NO – STAND UP FOR EUROPE**' said one, making reference to a Charlie McCreevy quote. '**MILKED DRY!**' claimed another one, with a picture of a cow above. As if the threat of milkless Friesians wasn't enough, they also invoked 1916, picturing Pearse, Clarke and Connolly with the headline '**THEY DIED FOR YOUR FREEDOM – DON'T THROW IT AWAY**'.

The point about Pearse et al. along with their apparent religious fervour obviously resonated with commenters on their site, one of them writing: 'Fair play to you for campaignin [sic] against this Godless treaty, They just want to take away our Holy God and replace Him with science. That too and the Fact that the Godless treaty will lead us to being swamped with asylum seakers [sic] and foreigners from Africa is this what Pearse gave his life for I ask you?'

Another commenter, seemingly concerned at the salty nature of the language in describing how many posters they'd put up, asked, ' … do we have to use words such as "Erected" on our About Us page?'

In terms of shrill bombast, the posters were almost beyond parody. Almost, but not quite. Pastiche posters spread like wildfire, with slogans like '**ONE IN THREE EUROPEANS HAS A MOUSTACHE VOTE NO**'.

After that it just snowballed, a deluge of Cóir mock-ups each more amusing and surreal than the last. Posters like that of the prostitute peering in a car window with the caption '**YOUR KIDS WILL GROW UP DUTCH!**' (which the *Evening Herald* accidentally thought was genuine) and one, presumably harking back to the 'Milked Dry' poster, that simply said, '**GOATS**'.

But despite the hours of fun to be had with Cóir,

the winner of the most outrageous poster award was everyone's favourite pan-European washout, Libertas.

With a cloudy, orangey sky as a background, and a crying wee girl with massive green eyes making an 'I want a pony!' face, the poster read 'IRISH DEMOCRACY, 1916 – 2009? VOTE NO!' Oh dear. In other words, either they genuinely thought Irish democracy started then and they've assembled their knowledge of Irish history from sugar packets, or they had in fact heard of Parnell and O'Connell, but just ignored them to make some daft romantic point. That's referenda for ye.

❖

Perpetual Embarrassment Rating: 10/10
Any political party putting forward the notion that Irish democracy started in 1916 is either full of amateurs or idiots. Or both.

National Peril-o-meter: 10/10
Our kids growing up Dutch? Not on my watch!

'Ah, lads!' Rating: 9/10
Why, oh why, can't people online who complain about foreigners coming to this country ever seem to spell properly?

The next proposed referendum:
Over whether we ever hold another referendum again.

They Went Where?!

The Time a Councillor Hid in the Bushes to Avoid the Po-leese

The correlation between our elected officials and automotive malfeasance really is as bewildering as it is terrifying. Whether it's Jim McDaid (see *The Time a Transport Minister Drove the Wrong Way Down a Dual Carriageway*), or Ming (see *The Time Ming Tried to Gain Brownie Points by Admitting the Guards Quashed His Penalty Points*), it seems power plus whatever they have in their systems goes to their heads in a pretty lethal way.

Take the case of Fine Gael Cork councillor Michael Hegarty. A well-regarded member of the council for over a quarter of a century and leader of Fine Gael's caucus in the chamber, Councillor Hegarty was driving happily along in his car one day when he saw a garda checkpoint in the near distance.

We've all been there, when we have that moment of panic on seeing a checkpoint and the internal checklist runs through your head: 'Did I leave my licence back at the house?' 'God, I remembered to update the tax disc, didn't I?' and so forth. And, in Councillor Hegarty's case, 'Am I drunk off my ass?'

The answer, at least to the last question, was yes. Yes he was.

Now as any motorist knows, the key to not being stopped by the rozzers at a checkpoint is acting like you really want to be. Roll down the window in advance, all smiles and waves and whatnot, and you're sure to be waved on through. But if you let your body and eyes tense up all shiftily, you'll have a high viz jacket all up in your window space. Guess which option Hegarty went for?

Well actually, he went for a third, much worse, option: a hilariously conspicuous attempt to evade the checkpoint. One of the guards said he saw 'a car approaching the checkpoint and stopping a short distance away at a junction. It turned suddenly to the left with a screech of wheels.'

At this point the guards gave chase in the squad car and, after no doubt crashing into some cardboard boxes along the way, Hegarty pulled into a churchyard, got out of his car, hopped a wall and hid in some bushes in the vain hope of evading capture. If at any stage he had wished he just had a Britvic before reaching for the keys, it was probably now.

Once the guards had intercepted the impromptu Bear

Grylls effort and he was taken in for being two times over the limit, Councillor Hegarty just couldn't stop clutching at the long grass. He claimed he was 'improperly deprived of his liberty' and that he shouldn't have been arrested on private property. He stopped just short of suggesting the bushes he was hiding in were parley, or that the guards hadn't counted to a hundred with their eyes closed before catching him.

The judge wasn't buying it, giving a two-year driving ban and a fine of €600. While still a councillor, Hegarty resigned his two major posts pertaining to council business. The first, his leadership of Fine Gael on the council, had more to do with the fact that he owed the Revenue about 80 grand. The second was a bit more to do with his speeding away from the gardai like he had a towbar made of cocaine and then hid from them in shrubbery. The post in question? Chairman of the Joint Policing Committee, naturally.

But that wasn't the end of it. In July 2013, the parley defence sort of worked. Hegarty's counsel won the 'improperly deprived of his liberty' argument, as the gardai made an error in obtaining the breathalyser: they put him in the back seat of the squad car while he took it. This, it was argued, was tantamount to unwarranted arrest. Despite having admitted to having four drinks, the judge was compelled to given him the benefit of the doubt over the validity of the detention and the conviction was flattened. Much like the bushes he was hiding from the guards in.

❖

Perpetual Embarrassment Rating: 8/10

First the drink, then the driving, then the chase, then the hiding from the guards. The embarrassment is layered like a wedding cake.

National Peril-o-meter: 4/10

Unless the parish groundskeeper getting a bollocking for having the gate open counts as national peril, negligible.

'Ah, lads!' Rating: 8/10

Policing committee chair causing a car chase is pretty bad, but he could have gone the whole hog and driven down a dual carriageway, like they do in those American car chases. Or the wrong way down it like Dr McDaid.

Hints for next time:

Just have a drink in the house. A lot less hassle, cops or leaves.

The Time George Lee
Paid a Flying Visit to the Dáil

I'll never forget where I was when I heard the news. It was the early summer of 2009, and I was in an internet café (2009 was a different time, man) when I got a text on my Nokia 3210 (I'm old-fashioned, OK?). 'Did you hear the news?' it read. 'George Lee's running for the Dáil.' AT LAST.

The country was stuck in a high-cycle spin in the washing machine of international economics, and people were crying out for a change, a bit of colour, a hero, goddammit. And what could be more colourful or heroic than the top man of the RTÉ Economics Department?

You might think I'm being overly sarcastic, but he really was that popular. When he came to NUIG to speak a few months after running, the place was packed out. Despite the omnipresent George Lee being the most overworked man in a country saturated in economic woe, rather than shooting the messenger, the public sort of came to love him. And so, when Seamus Brennan died and his seat became vacant, Fine Gael pulled a masterstroke by asking George to stand for the seat. He ran, saying that in the context of Ireland's unprecedented economic disaster, he couldn't look his grandkids in the face and say he did nothing to try and fix it.

Step 1 went well. Very well. He didn't just win the seat, he demolished allcomers, winning over 27,000 votes and a cool 53 per cent. So, with his enormous public mandate, his popular reputation as a good communicator and a man who knew his economic onions in a party that was destined for government any time now, surely he was the one to cut through the usual politicians' treacle and solve these problems with both barrels? Eh …

Nine months into his fledgling career, it didn't quite take. He seemed to spend his time in the Dáil as equal parts valuable figurehead, and intern that nobody knew what work to give to. He said he had 'virtually no input or influence' and had only met then Finance spokesman Richard Bruton a handful of times, a situation unlikely to have happened had he still been economics editor at RTÉ. He was given chairmanship of a forum on the economy, but Lee himself said he had not been consulted before being given what seemed to be nothing more than a sinecure.

He added, 'Although a role may well have been

provided, I believe from my point of view it is too late. Nine months is a long time.'

Nine months may be a long time in the world of 24-hour news, but in politics that's only a couple of committee meetings.

The role that 'may well have been provided' was a reference to Enda Kenny's reaction to the matter. He claimed he anticipated George being an important part of the party's future economic plans, essentially the equivalent of 'But George, we didn't forget your birthday, we had a cake here waiting for you!' Kenny even promised him an immediate promotion to the front bench, but George wasn't looking for a concession, he was looking for his way out.

The reaction to Lee's premature check-out was mixed. Some within Fine Gael, like Michael Noonan, didn't seem to realise there was a problem and thought he was settling in fine. Lucinda Creighton on the other hand was more critical, suggesting the party could have done more to bring him into the fray. Outside the beltway, opinion was split as to whether Lee was being petulant and weak of resolve, or whether politics is just an impregnable field for a norm like him. Within a few months Lee was back at RTÉ, his political career like one of those really vivid dreams where you scan your tongue round your mouth to make sure your teeth didn't actually fall out. One big effect he did have though was to start Fine Gael's Night of the Long Butter Knives against Enda Kenny, the one that nearly toppled him but not quite (see *The Time Fine Gael Plotted against Their Leader Really Badly*). Another important thing he contributed to was paving the way for the Dáil career of Peter Matthews, who succeeded him in getting the third Fine Gael seat at the next election. Peter Matthews. How will we explain that to the grandchildren?

❖

Perpetual Embarrassment Rating: 7/10
Nobody came out of it looking well: George Lee for his lack of stamina, Fine Gael for their lack of giving George Lee a proper job.

National Peril-o-meter: 7/10
It nearly put paid to Enda Kenny's leadership, and what would we have done then?

'Ah, lads!' Rating: 8/10
How is it Leo Varadkar became a frontbench spokesman almost immediately when entering the Dáil but George Lee was left to stew on the backbenches for nine months?

People who spent a fortune kitting their car out with stickers saying 'I'm for George Lee':
Must have been pretty pissed.

The Time Boris
Yeltsin Never Saw Shannon

We've had bigger visitors (Big Dog Clinton in 1995, for example), but in September 1994 everyone's favourite boogying President of Russia Boris Yeltsin was due to make a quick stop at Shannon on the way back from Washington, and so Taoiseach of the time Big Al Reynolds and a host of dignitaries replete with their best telephone voices assembled at the airport, where the tarmac had no doubt been given a burst with a hydraulic hose, and the red carpet a quick shampooing.

So there they all were, waiting around when the plane came in sight, heads filled with questions such as 'I wonder what he's like?' 'Do you reckon he'll dance at this thing?' 'Reckon I could beat him at a shot-drinking contest?' 'I wonder what's on the menu for this reception tonight?' and the like. But one of the questions they probably didn't expect to ask themselves was, 'Eh, why is his plane flying round and around like that?'

Seeing such strange airline antics must have caused Big Al something of a flashback. In his early political career, having made a fortune from the notoriously lucrative dual enterprises of dancehalls and pet food, he became embroiled in a nightmare scenario while Minister for Transport in 1981. An Aer Lingus plane was hijacked on its way from Dublin to London, putting Reynolds front and centre of the rescue mission. Except it wasn't quite your usual hijacking. A poker-faced Reynolds gave a 'maybe I know stuff, maybe I don't' briefing to the press, but did reveal he suspected the hijacker to be Irish. When a journalist asked if he had any demands, Reynolds, fully aware that what he was about to say was preposterous, divulged that the hijacker demanded the publishing of the Third Secret of Fatima.

'It's a religious secret,' Reynolds said, 'it's not for me to say what it is.'

At any rate, the plane was diverted to France where French special forces stormed it. They were able to do so because the hijacker didn't see the lights indicating the doors had been breached in the cockpit. Moriarty he weren't.

Zooming back to 1994 and Reynolds was now Taoiseach, albeit a rather unlikely one. The public's thoughts were summed up by one Dermot Morgan, who in an enduring sketch claimed, 'The one thing you have to bear in mind with Albert Reynolds is the phrase "rabbit in the headlights" … he embarrasses me, he makes me

fearful, I know he's going to commit the ultimate faux pas', before suggesting he'd ask the Indian PM what his cut at the door of the Taj Mahal was.

The characterisation of the 'country and western Taoiseach' who ran the country like a bank holiday hooley stuck. Even when it wasn't his fault, Reynolds and a vague hapless feeling seemed to go hand in hand, and

Yeltsin's circling over Shannon was a case in point. After about half an hour of just hovering about, the Russian plane eventually landed, but that wasn't the end of the daftness. Another quarter of an hour passed before poor Albert was received by the Deputy Prime Minister, who said that Boris was not well. And very tired. And there was something in his eye and the dog ate his homework. Well, not the last one.

What was suggested afterwards though was that Boris got a bit polluted on the plane at Shannon for all the pizzazz of a diplomatic event, as he was simply too pizzed off his azz to get off. Yeltsin later insisted that he had simply been sleeping heavily and none of his security detail dared wake him. 'I'll give them a kick for that,' he said jovially. It's just a shame they weren't meeting him in Kerry, otherwise he'd probably have been allowed to fly the plane (see *The Time the Healy-Rae Brothers Tried to Revolutionise Irish Transport*).

❖

Perpetual Embarrassment Rating: 6/10
Boris was always doing crazy stuff like this, and Albert lived in a sort of semi-embarrassed haze anyway.

National Peril-o-meter: 3/10
The only potentially dangerous thing was the pilot getting dizzy flying round so much.

'Ah, lads!' Rating: 8/10

Did the Russians think nothing of the fact that we had a big spread of Kimberleys and Mikados in the airport at all at all?

Strength of the vodka on board: 8/10.

Eh, allegedly.

The Time Michael Lowry Wanted To Be Mr Burns

Having a book featuring the ludicrous-but-true of Irish politics without making reference to Michael Lowry would be like having a birthday party and cake, but forgetting to bring plates or knives and forks. Or icing. Or a cake.

The story that springs immediately to mind involving Lowry is of course The Perfectly Above-Board Granting of a Mobile Licence back in the 1990s, his expulsion from cabinet and the Fine Gael party as a result of it being mere jealousy. Also, his settling up with the Revenue to the tune of seven figures? Jealousy. And the damning Moriarty Tribunal findings against him, and subsequent campaign to get him to resign? Media jealousy. That's the worst kind of jealousy.

Themmuns up in Dublin might not get him, but the salty people of North Tipperary (that's the right phrase, isn't it?) get him, and they've been stuck with him, I mean stuck by him, for years. In fact they've had him as an Independent TD for nearly twice as long as he was a Fine Gael TD or a government minister. Why? To make reference to David McSavage's best-known quote, 'He fiksched the road.'

Lowry belongs to a very particular type of politician, the local fixer, the fief (that's 'f-i-e-f', in case any lawyers are reading), the *capo di tutti capi* of the few dozen townlands he surveys. The type who have 'going on the canvass' down to an art. Not for him the lattes, smartphones and national legislation of Dublin 4. For Lowry and those like him, the Dáil is useful only for securing stuff for your constituency, so every five years you can point to some school, swimming pool or community centre and nod and wink to people that you were responsible. It's a bit like an indolent hanger-on standing close behind someone giving a present, in the hope the recipient will think it's from both of them.

But with all the stories floating around about Lowry over the years, this one most uncannily sums up the man's vain, bombastic boondoggling: the Grand Tipperary Casino Project.

It all started in May 2011, when Abbeygreen Consulting Ltd bought a site near the preposterously named Two Mile Borris. Michael Lowry was, *quelle surprise*, a director of the buyers. Queller surprise, he didn't put that on his register of interests in the Dáil.

He remembered rightly to lobby for the thing, though,

and just a month later the whole thing was given the 'Feck it, sure why not?' by An Bord Pleanála. In a plan straight out of *The Simpsons'* Monty Burns Casino episode, the proposal involved a 500-bedroom hotel with health spa and swimming pool, two ballrooms, two bars, four restaurants, six retail units, and a conference centre in a pear tree. Oh, and of course the casino. In the middle of bloody Tipperary.

But wait, there's more! They also planned to build a banqueting suite and museum that was a replica of the bloody White House, as well as having a replica Lafayette Gardens to boot. But if a little bit of 1600 Pennsylvania Avenue in the middle of nowhere wasn't enough for you, how about an all-weather racecourse and dog track with 20,000 capacity between them, replete with stables and kennels and an equestrian centre? Or a semi-domed music venue with a retractable roof that could hold 15,000? Or a golf course and driving range? Or 20 motherflipping retail outlets, just for the craic?

If only that was the end of it. Also proposed were a heliport, a single-storey energy centre and water treatment plant (because not everything can be sexy, I guess) and, since no casino would be complete without it, a chapel. This is presumably so Elvis could officiate weddings there. Or failing that, where poor sods could go and ask, 'Jesus Christ almighty, how am I going to get that money back?!'

At best, it was outrageously ambitious. At worst, it would have made Citizen Kane cringe.

Lowry may have softened up some ground and been a public champion for the cause, but the brains of the operation and magic man pulling the white elephant out of the hat was Richard Quirke, the man behind Dr Quirkey's Goodtime Emporium on Dublin's O'Connell Street, although the validity of his claims of having gone to Goodtime Medical School are flimsy at best. Quirke thought that the best way for Ireland to rally back from the blight of reckless, unsustainable, illogical gambling and hubristic indulgence was to build a shiny, garish monument to all those things. But hey, job creation is job creation, right?

Austin Broderick of the Thurles Chamber of Commerce certainly seemed to think so, elegantly putting it, 'If a Chinaman came in, or some other man came in, and said he was going to give 2,000 jobs to the area here … We'd meet him with a red carpet and open arms.'

The lamentably un-Chinese Quirke was pretty reticent about talking about his grand scheme to journalists, which Michael Lowry was quick to defend: 'What divine right have you to have Richard Quirke stand in front of you or answer your questions? Richard Quirke is a businessman. He makes investment decisions on his own behalf and if Richard Quirke is not available to you, that's his business.'

The wheels started to come off when, despite An Bord Pleanála's green light, the proposed music venue was vetoed, thereby stopping the concern's dream of getting Beyoncé to say 'Hello, Tipperary!' The final, more decisive blow came several months later when the cabinet decided that there would be no change in the law, as required to facilitate such a project, as the Taoiseach was mindful of protecting the young and vulnerable when it came to gambling. Michael Lowry said he was 'surprised and disappointed' by the decision. Meanwhile, for the upcoming Gambling Bill he was preparing, Alan Shatter said he didn't think super casinos were in the public interest and the bill would speak to facilitate smaller, more modest casinos.

'Modest casinos'. See, that's where they went wrong.

❖

Perpetual Embarrassment Rating: 9/10
I just can't help believing that a Vegas-style casino is a terrible, gaudy idea.

National Peril-o-meter: 7/10
The way the Thurles Chamber of Commerce talked, you'd think not having the casino would turn the place into the ghetto.

'Ah, lads!' Rating: 8/10
Lowry and Quirke are hardly the devil in disguise, but they certainly had Ireland's anti-gambling caucus all shook up.

Did you think you'd get away with all those Elvis puns?
Uh huh huh.

The Time a New TD
Went Grand Theft Auto
at the Dáil

Brand new TDs often try hard to make their presence felt on their first day, for better or worse. Go-getters like Dr Noël Browne, Martin O'Donoghue and Niamh Breathnach were made ministers on their very first day in the Dáil, while Oliver J. Flanagan was reprimanded by the Ceann Comhairle for being 'persistently irrelevant' during his maiden speech. And lct's not forget Pee Flynn, who showed up for his first day at work in a typically ostentatious, Johnny Logan-esque white suit (see *The Time Pee Flynn Went to the Zoo on Live TV*).

But Mary Mitchell O'Connor's debut at the Dáil took the biscuit. Or, rather, the suspension off her car. It had been a circuitous route to the Dáil for Mitchell O'Connor. She was elected a councillor for the Progressive Democrats in 2004, but jumped ship in late 2007 to Fine Gael, believing the PDs had no future. They might not have had any prospects, but Mary did, as she went on to be comfortably elected in 2009 and chosen as Sean Barrett's running mate for the 2011 election. Despite it being a tough four-seater constituency with a lot of well-known names contesting, a mix of careful vote management and Fine Gael's rating being so high they needed breathing equipment ensured she won a seat. All that was left was to enjoy her first day in the Dáil, get to know the place and do nothing embarrassing. What could possibly go wrong?

Like *Downton Abbey*, an automotive mishap at the end sort of spoiled the whole thing. Coming out of the car park, Mary made a wrong turn and drove her bright red Hyundai – still replete with election stickers that had her face on them – down the plinth at the front of Leinster House. Inevitably, there were reporters and photographers present, who were in hysterics laughing at her slide down the bannister. At one point, someone shouted the searingly obvious 'Take a picture!' as she drove out the gate, mercifully with her bumper not causing sparks on the floor.

But Mary, described once by *The Irish Times* as 'beautifully turned out' (not a comment Pee Flynn would be likely to get – or, indeed, any male politician), is a shining example of that old proverb, 'When life gives you stairs, make a tremulous first gear getaway.' I may be paraphrasing. She went on Matt Cooper's show the day after to give a light-hearted interview, saying she'd booked an appointment with the optician and the only injury she endured was to her pride. And, suggesting she's a student of Bill Clinton's 'triangulation' policy to beat opponents to the punch, her website's slogan is 'Crossing the plinth of Irish politics'. Nice. Although, still having it on your website two years later doesn't exactly make it likely people will forget any time soon.

Incidentally, the very day this all happened was also the day Europe announced that cheaper female-only insurance premiums would be ended.

❖

Perpetual Embarrassment Rating: 8/10

Had she been leaving at nine at night and nobody out at the gates, she probably wouldn't have driven anywhere near the plinth.

National Peril-o-meter: 4/10

If any sort of vehicle was ever to storm the Dáil, it's unlikely to be a red Hyundai saloon.

'Ah, lads!' Rating: 4/10

Hey, it could happen to anybody. And I'm not just saying this because I once took the mirror off a van in front of a large group of people.

Grace under fire: 9/10

Credit it to her, the woman knows how to take a joke. And indeed, still taking it two years later.

The Time Ming Tried to Gain Brownie Points by Admitting the Guards Quashed His Penalty Points

'There was a time when the police in this country were friends of the Church; speeding tickets torn up, drunk-driving charges quashed, even a blind eye turned to the odd murder!'

Father Ted Crilly may have fulminated against the loss of priestly perks, but it seems for some in Irish life the boys in blue are still more than happy to help luminaries out of a hole. The traffic stuff, that is, the murder not so much. One such recipient of that garda gratuity was the idiosyncratic Roscommon/South Leitrim TD Luke 'Ming' Flanagan, although true to form, his reaction was most unusual.

On a scale of dramatic divorce not seen since Richard Burton and Liz Taylor, Ming's parting from reality

resulted in him making statements that variously made him judge, jury and transgressor, like Elliot Ness stopping by Al Capone's swinging hotspot for a few bevvies after a hard day gang-busting with his Untouchables.

Back in 1997, Ming was anything but mainstream. He ran for election in Galway West on a strident pro-legalising cannabis platform, boasting posters in which he looked like Huggy Bear. He wasn't just a one-trick pony, though, as he also advocated an end to 'Deliberate treatment like shit by Social Welfare system of its dependants' and a wish to address 'Failure by system to enforce the Housing Regulation Act'. The last one is particularly interesting, as it was a swipe from his landlord at the time, one Frank Fahey, TD, who Ming claimed had not registered his house for rent. Despite this, he ran for Fianna Fáil on their hilarious-in-hindsight zero tolerance to crime platform in 1997. As Luke once commented in explanation on the historically invaluable Irish Election Literature blog, 'People in glass houses and all that.' Little did he know that in a few years he'd be moving out of Frank's house and walking into a glass gaffe of his own.

It all started around Christmas 2012, when a band of backbench banditos including Ming held a press conference in which they called serious shenanigans on garda practice. It appeared the guards were still very much of the kind that Ted Crilly remembered, with Mick Wallace claiming, 'We have evidence of anywhere between 60,000 and 100,000 episodes of it … the termination of penalty points is widespread.' So widespread, in fact, at least one such episode was sitting feet away.

On two separate occasions, Ming had penalty points quashed himself. The first instance was after he was caught on the mobile by a garda sergeant – he was told he could have his points removed because he was on his way to the Dáil, if he wrote a letter indicating as much. The second time he was at a meeting in Roscommon and when he relayed that he'd been caught driving while on the phone again to officials, presto chango, they were gone again. Except he didn't mention this to anyone.

In fact, he out and out denied it around Christmas when a person on Twitter asked him explicitly, even going as far as to say, 'Are you sure?'

Ming replied, 'Certain, why you ask?'

To his credit (kind of), he didn't deny or equivocate getting the kind of preferable treatment he dubbed as corrupt, he just didn't seem to realise he had any part in it. To him, he had this foisted upon him, and sure what could he do about it? And explaining his reticence in admitting he had points quashed, indeed being abjectly untruthful about it, he suggested it was his plan all along and he's been wearing a wire for the past few months.

Vincent Browne led the charge of the flabbergasted on his show, along with Fine Gael TD Joe O'Reilly (who, in the most fantastic case of Hope Springs Eternal, once accidentally sent out leaflets saying 'Senator Joe O'Reilly TD') playing the role of disappointed uncle, and *Daily Mail* journalist Niamh Lyons, who could make you burst into tears after a few minutes of extended staring. Vincent hammered away, stating Ming colluded in and instigated the corruption. Ming insisted he didn't, as the garda sergeant approached him first, presumably with a lamp shining in his face, forcing him to write it. Vincent, over the noise of his throbbing head vein, then countered that he absolutely instigated it. Ming responded with the phrase that kills every argument stone frustratingly dead: 'Well, that's your opinion.'

An exasperated Browne told him, 'God, you're in serious denial!' and 'You've dug some big hole for yourself'. Ming predictably denied this, shouting up from the bottom of the mine shaft he crafted. The salient point of Ming's refusal to name the official who got the second batch of points removed then came up. Uncle Joe said that in all his years he'd never met an official who would do that and that he would need to name him, so as to let the other county executives who don't act like lads who sell watches from the inside of their overcoat off the hook. Ming said it was up to the official. And when asked why he kept his undercover work to himself, he explained, 'I didn't think there was any mileage out of it … or that anyone would listen.'

Niamh Lyons artfully completed the broiling by pointing out that many people get points expunged for quite legitimate reasons like speeding en route to a maternity ward, and that those people all go on a register explaining the circumstances. And since Ming sunk the boot in pretty hard to those people as well as the legitimate transgressors, he probably shouldn't continue as part of the campaign.

She also got him to admit that what he availed of was corrupt, so much so that now it was out there he wanted the points back, because 'I clearly deserve them.' At this point, all Vincent could summon was, 'But, but, but!'

So bad was Ming's performance that his dysfunctional backbench family in the Independent Technical Group thought about removing him from it, as he was 'damaging the brand'. Knowing them, the group probably owns an actual iron.

❖

Perpetual Embarrassment Rating: 2/10
Embarrassing? Well, that's your opinion …

National Peril-o-meter: 7/10
Casting aspersions on the guards isn't a great way to make you a legislator of renown. Especially when they've gone to such trouble to help you out.

'Ah, lads!' Rating: 9/10
Decrying behaviour you secretly benefit from is suit-and-tie-at-a-dinner-dance stuff, not Sesame-Street-shirt-goatee-beard stuff.

Vincent Browne rage grade:
B+. Bear in mind, though, an A grade involves weaponry.

The Time Michael Ring Was Attacked by a Giant Inflatable Penis

If for whatever reason a massive scrap were to break out in the Dáil (it's only a matter of time, surely), then there's only one person I'd be putting my money on to emerge victorious from any such battle royal: Michael Ring.

Few people have ever walked through Leinster House as fearsome as The Ring. A prodigious vote-getter with an argumentative style that could corrode steel, if Michael Ring was around in ancient times, the kraken would be legging it in the opposite direction.

Battle-hardened on Mayo County Council and Westport Urban District Council, he was promoted to the big leagues in 1994. There, he showed his fearlessness early on by putting Beverley 'Class Act' Flynn to the sword in the by-election to replace her own father. Once elected, he was less a TD in the traditional sense and more an all-powerful Western sheriff, cultivating a stupefying vote base. One of the ways he would do this was through attending funerals. All of them. So prolific is he, some in the area reckon he must have a map on his wall like that in a cop show, with his wife as the logistics manager making sure he can get to as many as he can. It's even inspired a very western aphorism: 'You're not officially dead in Mayo until Michael Ring offers his condolences.'

His helicopter mourning and reputation around Westport as their man in the capital meant he topped the poll twice on the trot in 1997 and 2002, trouncing one Enda Kenny in the process. His 2002 result was especially impressive, as Fine Gael were electorally stripped to their jocks that particular year. Only when Enda became party leader did he eventually overtake Ring as the chief vote-getter in Mayo, but even then he was always run incredibly close by the man *Magill* magazine once dubbed 'Heckler of the Year'. Small wonder, when one of his most famous Dáil showdowns was with Ceann Comhairle John 'I Am the Law!' O'Donoghue, where he was thrown out for shouting 'He's making it up as he goes along!' to The Great Robed One.

Enda must have got a fair barracking then when he controversially decided to throw Ring out of his deck during a reshuffle in 2004. But, as having an angry Michael Ring in your ranks is as dangerous as a remote control chainsaw, when Fine Gael got into government after the election in 2011 he was given the plum role of

Minister of State for Tourism and Sport. No doubt, it was an incident on the campaign trail for that election that convinced the new Taoiseach that Michael was the right man to be managing the many throngs wanting to come to Ireland. Namely, his good humour when photographed with a massive inflatable throng.

Apart from being very tidy and the ideal place to live in Ireland, Westport is also known as a bit of a hotspot for hen parties. For all his local knowledge, Ring hadn't planned on one of said hen parties getting up close and personal one evening when he was being accompanied by the *Irish Times* sketch writer Miriam Lord. Some of the revellers obviously recognised him, and in a way only a tanked-up person in the throes of a party can do, went, 'Michael, will ye come out?' For a photo presumably, not out to the Castlecourt for a few Jägerbombs. Fair enough, apart from the fact that the woman asking the question was pushing an inflatable penis through the window of his car as she did it. When lobbing it through the passenger window didn't work, she and her precious cargo raced round the other side to Michael. Since they never tell you how to deal with such things in Dáil School, Michael Ring made the best of the situation, opened the door and posed for photos with the hen party, including their additional member. Miriam Lord, meanwhile, didn't know where to look. Well, she knew exactly where to look, she just didn't.

❖

Perpetual Embarrassment Rating: 4/10

Frankly, if you were in Westport for the weekend and didn't have such an altercation, something would be badly wrong.

National Peril-o-meter:

See above.

'Ah, lads!' Rating: 3/10

Michael was probably just glad to have 'TD' and 'big prick' used in a very different context than usual.

Miriam Lord's inflatable penis flashbacks:

None to my knowledge.

The Time a Transport Minister Drove the Wrong Way Down a Dual Carriageway

You get the impression when Dr James McDaid rocked up to the Dáil for the first time, he did so Don Johnson-style in a red Ferrari, rolled up sleeves on his jacket with pastel coloured T-shirt underneath, that song from *Ferris Bueller's Day Off* (the one that goes OH YEAH! in slow motion) booming from his car radio. In over 20 years in the Dáil, McDaid time and again proved himself to be a renegade maverick who played by his own rules. Sure, the captain downtown thought he was reckless, and the DA was always busting his ass, but he got results dammit, and the people of Letterkenny loved him. And so, apparently, did the ladies.

Charles Haughey, presumably seeing this wavy-haired roustabout on the backbenches and sensing a kindred spirit, elevated him to the front bench after a mere two years, making him Minister for Defence in 1991. For, like, three minutes.

The very morning he was appointed Minister for Defence, a photo came to light that featured McDaid smiling in the background on the day Maze Prison escapee James Clarke evaded extradition at the Four Courts. The Progressive Democrats got spooked at the notion Óglaigh na hÉireann would be run by an apparent Provo sympathiser, and so McDaid was booted off the case. He wouldn't get his government badge and holster back for another six years.

But when he did, boy was he in his element. He was appointed Minister for Sport, Tourism and Recreation, and what could be better than going to the beach or the ball game in the name of work? And while conventional wisdom up in Donegal suggests that kids there had never seen a proper goalpost prior to the Ministry of The Good Doctor, it was the Recreation end of the gig that ended up getting the most attention. McDaid earned himself the epithet 'Minister for Fun', and his rumoured relationship with Anne Doyle turned the nation into eavesdropping Carry On characters.

But in 2002, the Ministry of Fun was taken off him, and it was here that it started going less Don Johnson and more Nick Nolte.

In a forum prior to the election in 2002 he referred to suicide victims as 'selfish bastards', a particularly daft comment for a medical doctor to make. Even though he'd lost his front-bench seat and was developing an unfortunate propensity for attracting all the wrong kind of attention, he managed to hold on to a ministerial posting, as the number two man at the Department of Transport. For two years he avoided any kind of embarrassing automotive disaster. If only he could have said the same once he returned to the backbenches.

It all started so well in 2002, when he spearheaded a drink-driving campaign, saying, 'Some drivers still choose to ignore our drink-driving laws and as a result innocent lives are destroyed.'

Fast forward to 2005. After a long day's indulgence and generally being James McDaid at a race meeting at Punchestown, he was taken by helicopter back to Dublin, because his life wasn't enough like a Duran Duran video to begin with. No doubt owing to his profound sozzlement, he ignored a handful of fate lifeboats: he was offered a room for the night at the City West Hotel, and evaded a taxi ordered for him so he could drive his own car back. He soon went the wrong way round the Newhall Roundabout, and subsequently drove the wrong way down the Naas dual carriageway. Several cars and even an ambulance angrily remonstrated with him, and it was only when a lorry jack-knifed itself on purpose at a roundabout that he was stopped. The lorry driver took his keys, and the plain-clothes garda who was following him took him in, where he was discovered to be three times over the then legal limit. 2002 Safety Launch Jim would have been appalled.

As is often the case, the difference between a funny story and disaster can often be a couple of inches, and so it was that reaction to McDaid's high-speed capers was stifled laughter followed by white-hot fury. The whole thing was especially embarrassing as Bertie Ahern had recently made an appeal for people to take it handy on the roads and not do anything too stupid. You would therefore think that McDaid was bang to rights, but hey, this was a Fianna Fáiler in the mid-noughties, and blamelessness was totally in vogue.

Maverick to the end, with McDaid on the backbenches and his national lustre waning, he limited his various sound-offs to local media, although the nationals' ears did prick up again when he announced he wouldn't be relinquishing his pension. At one point he announced his retirement but came back because the good folk of Letterkenny would simply have missed him too much. Although given his desultory Dáil attendance record, it's a wonder they didn't miss him while he was actually there.

Turns out that towards the end of his Dáil career, McDaid acted like a man who was representing Brigadoon, only showing up for votes 17 per cent of the time, rock bottom of the Dáil hit parade. After promising to retire again before the 2011 election, he actually bailed out early when, with one eye no doubt on his medical practice, he resigned from the Dáil over de-funding of the HPV scheme. Imperfect though his career was, at least he didn't end it on a U-turn.

❖

Perpetual Embarrassment Rating: 10/10
I wonder did they take any of those side-profile pictures with him holding a slate with his name on it, like in the movies?

National Peril-o-meter: 10/10
All messing aside, it could have got seriously bad on so many levels.

'Ah, lads!' Rating: 10/10
Hard to know what's worse: a former Transport minister driving the wrong way up a dual carriageway, a man who fronted a drink-driving campaign three times over the limit, or a medical doctor getting an angry siren blast from an ambulance.

The wine at the Punchestown Races:
Strong, full-bodied and with notes of vanilla and sozzled ex-minister.

The Time Limerick Was Allowed to Drink but Nobody Else Was

Good Friday drinking is a classic example of how a low-impact issue can escalate into a polarising bar room brawl in a matter of seconds. Ireland's time-honoured tradition of knocking each other rotten in an off-licence on Holy Thursday started with the Intoxicating Liquor Act of 1927, which set aside Good Friday, Christmas Day and, laughably enough, Saint Patrick's Day as days where landlords all over the country would stand down from their levers. But as the country got a bit less pious and a bit more questioning, and the connection between sport, alcohol and big money got positively massive, Good Friday's status became a perennial debate. Fitting, then, that the most recent and notorious battle lines drawn between the old ways and 24-hour drinking freedom modernity also involved a fearsome rivalry: that of Leinster and Munster rugby.

In 2010, with a Celtic League match between the provinces falling on Good Friday thanks to Easter's notoriously flaky yearly schedule, and with attempts to change the match date failing, organisers faced a conundrum. A sell-out crowd of 26,000 was expected, as were several international reporters, all of whom would be wanting a sup no doubt and not all that concerned with the niceties of Irish intoxication law.

Pub owners reckoned several million quid could be lost in business, but they couldn't quite convince the gardai or the State, and took the issue to a judge on the grounds that this was a 'special event'. TO THE COURTS!

In court, Judge Tom O'Donnell held sway during a tug-of-love custody battle over the definition of a 'special event'.

'That is the real nub of the matter,' claimed Michael Murray, counsel for the State.

On nubs at least both sides were unanimous, as counsel for the vintners, Gearoid McGann, concurred that the special event status was 'the central nub' of the matter, and he went to great pains to so define it.

So reported *The Irish Times*: 'Mr McGann told the court that no legal definition existed to explain what a special event is. He quoted case law on the matter, referring to historic actions concerning a mart and a dance. Mr McGann also gave Oxford dictionary definitions for the words.'

Having precedent, marts, dances, the dictionary and central nubs on their side, Judge O'Donnell came down on the side of the publicans. He reasoned that since Thomond Park had a special stadium licence anyway, it 'seemed absurd that pubs in the locality could not open for business as well'. He also cited the unusual reason of allowing drinking on health and safety grounds, 'when 26,000 people would be spilling out of Thomond Park immediately after the match', and so gave the go-ahead for pubs to open between six p.m. and eleven thirty p.m., as long as they were in and around Limerick city. The exemption also included the phrase 'not in the county borough of Dublin', presumably some kind of legalese gamesmanship for the visiting Leinster team.

The Church didn't oppose the ruling in court, but I sort of wish Brother Sean O'Connor of the Moyross Franciscan Friars had. He fumed, 'If you identify yourself as a Catholic, then you should be nowhere near Thomond Park or a pub on that day ... If you're going against God and making a public stand about it, then you are serving mammon over God. I don't care how much money you pull in, it will backfire on you on a spiritual level.'

The Telegraph was quick to pick up Limerick serving mammon (and indeed a range of fine ales) over God, as they ran with the headline 'Irish pubs to open on Good Friday as locals worship rugby'. Limerick T-shirt sellers went a bit further, featuring slogans like 'Mass Will Now Take Place in Thomond Park', and in a topical reference to Limerick's myriad abuse scandals, political resignations and internal sporting disputes, 'We have no bishop, no minister and no hurling team, but we can drink on Good Friday'. The verdict was hailed as a victory for common sense by the vintners, but the most entertaining and diverse debate on the whole decision came from that pantheon of common sense we call the Seanad.

Joe O'Toole was very much in favour: 'Everyone would be a winner and free will would prevail. The separation of Church and State would be maintained and we would render unto Munster the things that are Munster's and to God the things that are God's.' Although he didn't answer Jerry Buttimer's question, 'What about BOD?'

Notorious aide-de-camp for Jesus, Ronan Mullen, must have left his usual brimstone in his other trousers, as he was quite measured and contemplative: 'I would shed no tears if there was a change in this law, yet I wonder whether we would lose something. Something good can be achieved by drawing on the tradition of Good Friday.'

More surprising was the opinion of swashbuckling liberal David Norris, who blasted the notion squarely in the face: 'It is outrageous to schedule such a match on Good Friday. I am old enough to remember when Sunday was a day that was reverenced in this country. It is good for people to have a day of rest … I certainly do not join this populist rush to say we should open pubs and desecrate Good Friday.'

Top contributor award though goes to showband

supremo, God-fearing, lusciously maned, leader of the Senate Donie Cassidy: 'I fully support Good Friday, which is a special family day. Nothing, including the television rights of a foreign television station, should interfere with our way of celebrating the crucifixion of the good Lord on Good Friday. That should not be allowed. I fully support every colleague who uttered his or her beliefs and genuine concern about this. Hands off Good Friday and Christmas Day.'

I'd dearly love to think that 'hands off' remark was a clever reference to rugby rucking terminology, but I doubt it. Oh, and Munster won by a point.

❖

Perpetual Embarrassment Rating: 6/10
We couldn't switch the taps off and there foreigners coming over now!

National Peril-o-meter: 9/10
It's all fun and games until Jesus comes back and jars us all for having a pint.

'Ah, lads!' Rating: 7/10
Is serving mammon on Good Friday not good because you have to fast off meat? Oh …

Holy Thursday in a supermarket:
Still one of the most dangerous nights of the year.

The Time a Priest Built
an Airport in between Masses

A few years ago, I was chairing a hustings debate among Students' Union candidates at my alma mater, NUIG. At one point, channelling my best Dimbleby, Humphrys and Paxman, I put it to a presidential candidate from Mayo that one (if not more) of his policies was wholly unrealistic. His reply, while not verbatim, went roughly like this:

> *Well, we had a man from Mayo who was told once that what he was doing was unrealistic too, and that was Monsignor James Horan, and he went and built an airport.*

It was a pretty oblique reference to make given the context, but given Horan's propensity for the out-there, oddly fitting. For the parish priest of Knock wasn't content with a Mass a day and twice on Sundays and all the tea he could drink.

The monsignor, the best-known Horan in the world until the genesis of One Direction, is of course famous for his notion to build an airport on a bog. Like *Field of Dreams*, where Kevin Costner digs up his livelihood so some legendary baseball players, who are all quite dead, can keep their skills posthumously polished. It's not certain whether Mayo's Sam-winning team of 1951 ever came to the site, in ghost form or otherwise. But the airport was but the third component in his Holy Trinity of thoroughly mad ideas.

The first was in the mid-seventies when he scored the considerable achievement of building Knock Basilica, the Old Trafford of praying. The second was more of a PR coup, managing to get that nice new pope and notable Marian devotee John Paul II over to Knock on his visit to Ireland, on the centenary of the Virgin Mary asking for directions in Knock after getting lost while holidaying in Westport. But his best and last marked him out not just as an overachieving builder and PR man, but as a kind of mad Keynesian genius.

In 1981, the daddy of west of Ireland reporters, Jim Fahy, went on a sodden, miserable day to Knock, and asked Monsignor Horan, who was overseeing a phalanx of diggers, a not unreasonable question: 'What exactly is going on here?'

'What does it look like, we're building an airport!'

Horan responded.

His rationale was that in the midst of a paralysing recession, an airport would be invaluable in opening up the region to the rest of the world. He continued, wryly joking to Fahy (at least I think he was), 'And I hope the Department of Transport doesn't hear about it. Now don't tell them ... We've no money, but we're hoping to get it next week, or the week after.'

So Monsignor Horan, those problems in mind, called the go-to man when it came to matters of looking for a few bob and jocular hints of impropriety: Charles Haughey. They were big fans of each other, with Horan sending him an epic piece of flannel praising his 'style and flair', and going as far as to say, 'You are doing a magnificent job in all departments [even the Transport one that's not to know about airport?] and we are all proud of you as a Mayo man.'

Haughey, flattered to within an inch of his life, agreed funding for the airport, but the economic hawk killjoys of the Fine Gael/Labour government reversed it. A regular man would have been put off, but Horan instead took off. On a worldwide tour to raise funds, specifically. A massive raffle and four million quid later, he incredibly got the airport off the ground in October 1985, or rather the chartered plane to Rome that was in the airport off the ground. The following year, the airport was opened commercially. Horan claimed that the airport opening was 'The best day for Connacht in 100 years', which makes you wonder what was happening in Mayo in October 1885. Did Michael Davitt throw some mad parties I'm not aware of?

Monsignor Horan sadly died the same year as the airport opened to the public, in 1986, but since its inception Knock Airport has become a roaring success, with 685,000 visitors in 2012. It's been given a rebranding of late, now known as Ireland West Airport Knock, meaning it's one of the few airports Ryanair uses that has an accurate description of where it actually is.

Horan's influence doesn't just extend to building, PR and aviation, but theatre, in the form of a musical (sure why not?) based on the Knock Airport saga called *A Wing and a Prayer*, which sort of deserves a round of applause.

But Horan's influence doesn't just extend to building, PR, aviation or theatre, but sculpture. In May 2013, a brass statue of the monsignor was unveiled, and in a fitting tribute to his pull over various taoisigh down the years, Enda Kenny was a guest of honour. The chairman of the splendidly named Monsignor Horan Statue Committee however admitted that they hadn't quite paid for the statue yet, but he was confident they would in due course. Maybe next week, or the week after?

❖

Perpetual Embarrassment Rating: 1/10

Far from it, Mayo people are very proud of it. They may even use it to bring the next Sam Maguire-winning team back, assuming space travel isn't mastered by then.

National Peril-o-meter: 2/10

The Department of Transport might have given Father Horan a bollocking, but Haughey had frankly much more dangerous things going on.

'Ah, lads!' Rating: 9/10

There's something incredibly Irish about the idea of building a white elephant airport in a place where the moors would be if we had any. Less Irish of course is the fact it actually got built.

Box office prospects of a film about a plane of priests hijacked over Knock being saved by Father Wesley Snipes:

I can't see how it can fail.

Northern Exposure

The Time Donegal Was Represented by an Empty Chair for over a Year

Donegal has long resigned itself to the notion that it is 'The Forgotten County' of Ireland. For a time in 2010–11 it had a compelling case, as it seemed Brian Cowen was oblivious to the fact that Donegal's roster of TDs had been one short for a wee while. And by 'wee while', I mean 17 months. Granted, Donegal also provided the Tánaiste of the time, but that was something many in The Forgotten County wanted to purge from memory themselves (see *The Time Mary Coughlan Lost at Science and Other Stuff Too*).

To get to the bottom of Donegal's empty chair problem we have to go back to 2002, when MEP and possibly west Donegal's second-best-known person after Daniel O'Donnell, Pat 'The Cope' Gallagher, returned from Europe to take back a second seat for Fianna Fáil in the South West constituency. Incidentally, Pat 'The Cope' is so-called because his grandfather was a pioneer of the cooperative movement in Dungloe, and having a name like a prizefighter is cool.

For seven pretty happy years Pat The Cope was a junior minister, perennial vote hooverer and generally king of all he surveyed, enjoying an unparalleled reputation as a local politician who can 'sort you out', be it a pothole filled, an expedited passport or ten-pound weight loss. But then, in 2009, something happened: and his name was Declan Ganley.

With Ganley's behemoth pan-European project Libertas threatening to take as many as one seat in the upcoming European elections, and with Fianna Fáil's incumbent MEP Seán Ó Neachtain retiring, making their seat vulnerable, the party needed an old-school Thunderbird to take on this New Age hood. And while The Cope may not have a spaceship, what he did have was a family shop and a shaking hand made of platinum. In a year where the Fianna Fáil tide was very much out, Pat The Cope was a few thousand votes off topping the poll, while the Libertas Zeppelin deflated slowly. But here's where the problems started.

In a move that bore striking resemblance to the wider economic woe of the country, Pat's return to Brussels was robbing Peter to pay Paul. Sure, FF held their European seat, but in so doing they had to relinquish The Cope's

Dáil seat. And with an embattled Cowen managing a majority thinner than a wafer from Ebenezer Scrooge's ice cream truck, he was not well disposed to risking the Opposition gaining a member in a near-impossible by-election. So he waited.

And he waited.

Even though it was clear to anybody who hadn't been holidaying in a Martian cave what was going on, half a year later then-Chief Whip Pat Carey gave an interview saying that there was no ulterior motive in the vacancy. 'The government is extremely preoccupied with a range of very important issues which need the full focus of the government … that does not mean there will not be a by-election at an early date that will be decided in due course,' he said, suggesting that the government treated the vacancy like a parent deflecting a kid's request to go to the zoo.

He went on to give a surreal justification of allowing such a lengthy vacancy by saying '… Donegal is represented by four TDs, three senators, and the Tánaiste.'

Sure haven't they enough to be getting on with? He then took the justification in another, uniquely creative, direction, suggesting that the previous TD was basically still doing the job anyway: 'Pat the Cope is there as often as people who claim to be representing the area as best as possible.'

Not put off by Fianna Fáil's assurance that Donegal had loads of representation, even from people who weren't supposed to be, both the public and Opposition were getting fed up. Matters weren't helped by a further two vacancies arriving following Martin Cullen's resignation and George Lee's political bungee cord snapping back (see *The Time George Lee Paid a Flying Visit to the Dáil*), and it was at this point that Sinn Féin got the lawyers involved.

Pearse Doherty's case before the High Court was going to be a success one way or another, as he put everyone else on the back foot by looking like the only person who could actually be arsed to do anything about the vacancy, which would either bode well for the by-election or general, whichever came first. As it happened, it was the by-election, placing him right in pole position. After nearly a year and a half of havering, humming and hawing, Donegal South West would finally get a bit of attention. The only problem with that, however, was that the politicians of Donegal South West would also get a bit of attention.

In the ensuing by-election, Fianna Fáil's Brian Ó Domhnaill personally guaranteed that he could stop the IMF swooping in (spoiler alert: he didn't), while Frank McBrearty caused the temperature (and voices) of every room he was in to rise every time he made a statement, prompting Labour advisors to often reach for their collars. He was also responsible for the moment of the by-election when seeing a picture of a large wave on the front of *The Irish Times* on Vincent Browne's paper review he said, and I'm paraphrasing, 'See that wave? That's Labour in the election, that.'

Vincent didn't seem to appreciate the imagery.

That left Pearse Doherty, who thanks to his court petition was well in front anyway, in an unassailable position. And, with those extra months' advantage on the new class of 2011, allowed him to make a debut speech that caught a great deal of attention and even set him out as a potential new leader. For him at least, it was probably worth the year and a half wait.

❖

Perpetual Embarrassment Rating: 7/10
You have to feel sorry for a senator who thinks he can stop the IMF single-handedly, like he's a west Donegal He-Man.

National Peril-o-meter: 5/10
If they could have got away without filling the seat, they would have, but frankly the empty seats are a lot less dangerous.

'Ah, lads!' Rating: 9/10
One of the people Fianna Fáil wanted to contest the by-election caused by Pat The Cope's European victory? You guessed it, Pat The Cope.

Getting a handshake from The Cope:
It's like the first time you heard The Beatles, man.

The Time a DUP Councillor Told Rihanna to Put Them Away

If there's one thing the DUP love, with the obvious exception of Free Presbyterian carrot cake (its secret is that it's more orange than other cakes), it's moralising. After all, they were a party created by Ol' Brimstone Boots Ian Paisley, and most of them are so 'traditional' in their views they genuinely think gay people are just one step above the alien that burst out of John Hurt's stomach, and think the Giant's Causeway was an early evolution of StairMaster created by giants.

Though to give them credit, they're just as opposed to straight people who aren't married getting sexy as gay people, as the whole world found out when Rihanna came to Northern Ireland. Hotfooting it from Rio de Janeiro to Belfast (oh, the glamour!), she was making the video for her hit 'We Found Love', Northern Ireland presumably topping the list of places you could credibly call 'a hopeless place'. One of the locations was a field in Bangor, and not for the first time (see *The Time a Council Meeting Discussed Eminem*), a musician fell foul of local politicians.

Happily shooting away with the video in a cornfield, Rihanna was, as Rihanna will inevitably be, quite undressed. At this point the field's owner, farmer and DUP Alderman Alan Graham, was passing by on his tractor, as DUP men will inevitably be. Not liking this ungodly show of Caribbean flesh one wee bit, he engages the entourage and tells them as much. Really politely.

'Then it moved to another field and perhaps then I wasn't sure what was going to happen. I realised things were becoming inappropriate from my point of view and I asked the filming to stop. They did stop. The gentleman may not have been aware of my expectations, but he treated me in a very gentlemanly way.'

He added that he meant 'no ill will against Rihanna and her friends', even though he had no idea who she was, as 'I didn't know who was coming. If the name "Rihanna" had been mentioned, well, no disrespect but it wouldn't have meant anything. I'm afraid I'm a bit illiterate regarding these issues.'

And although they shook hands and let that be that, he did reiterate: 'From my point of view, it was my land, I have an ethos and I felt it was inappropriate ... Perhaps

RIHANNA MEETS the DUP

they could acquaint themselves with a greater God.'

Like who, Jay-Z?

Of course, with a story containing an international superstar, prudish farmers and exposed boobies, the news spread half way round the world before Rihanna could get a fleece on, or Alderman Graham could get the tractor turned.

One of the stranger reactions to the whole sartorial interface was that of Barbara Windsor (sure why not?), who went on the *Jeremy Vine* show on BBC Radio 2, which is a much more genteel, together version of *Liveline* with breaks for Hall & Oates tracks. She said, perhaps mistaking Jeremy for Joe Duffy, 'It's a disgrace. I saw it this morning. I don't blame him. How old is he?

Does he need that at his time of life, seeing Rihanna taking her top off? He doesn't.'

Okey dokey …

When Jeremy asked her quite pertinently about her synonymy with exposed breasts, she responded, 'I got paid for that. That was a film made for artistic purposes. That was filmed in a muddy field at the back of the studios in a freezing November.'

Ah, well that's alright then

❖

Perpetual Embarrassment Rating: 8/10
Approaching Rihanna is not something many people get to do. Asking her to put more clothes on once you do is all but unprecedented.

National Peril-o-meter: 2/10
Not high, but the Babs Windsor rating in this story is by far the highest in the book.

'Ah, lads!' Rating: 3/10
In fairness, his field, his rules. His crazy, crazy rules.

Chances of Calvin Harris mixing a Free Presbyterian album of organ music:
Slim.

The Time Willie Frazer Fundamentally Confused Ireland and Italy

Come gather, ye young and old, for a story of a modern folk hero. A man who fights for freedom and justice. A man who's not afraid to take on powerful interests against insurmountable odds. A man who can look common sense in the face, and stare it down. A man who flies the flag for righteousness, and insists it flies every day, as long as that flag is red, white and blue. Behold, the hero of Ulster's flag saga, or indeed fleg sega.

He was born in 1960 and therefore I like to think his quest for things to be All British, All the Time was forged by the red hot embers of Roger Moore-era Bond films. Films like *The Spy Who Loved Me*, the opening of which features James embroiled in a ski chase (Alan Partridge describes this so much better than I do) and appearing to run off the edge of a cliff before unleashing his Union flag parachute, and Carly Simon alluding to his unrivalled status at 'it' (whatever 'it' is) over some silhouetted ladies. The name's Frazer. Willie Frazer.

Such visions of ostentatious patriotism and ludicrous freefall have been part of Willie Frazer's shtick for years. He set up FAIR, Families Acting for Innocent Relatives, following his own family's traumatic history of paramilitary violence, but also once claimed loyalist paramilitaries should never have been locked up in the first place and claimed he had a lot of time for loyalist commando Billy Wright. He ended up leaving FAIR after it had its funding revoked by the EU for the wonderfully Crilly-esque reason of 'major failures in the organisation's ability to adhere to the conditions associated with its funding allocation'. He was the man behind Dublin's notorious Love Ulster parade, where slabs of concrete and Charlie Bird got seriously roughed up. In 2007 he picketed Martin McGuinness' house to demand Libya pay compensation for victims of Troubles violence (sure why not?) but it didn't last long as he was harangued by McGuinness' Bogside neighbours and left after fifteen minutes.

But it was 2012 when Willie's folk heroism really moved into the big leagues. While passing through Donaghmore in County Tyrone, he saw a tricolour flag flying outside Saint Patrick's National School. Like a Protestant Popeye, that was all he could stands, he could stands no more, and he took to his Facebook page to register his outrage – OUTRAGE! – at the whole situation. With a wanton disregard for what The Man thought, or indeed for punctuation, he wrote, with accompanying photo: 'This is a school in Tyrone flying the Irish flag on the school grounds why.'

He then offered an answer to his own question: it was a prep school for precocious terrorists. According to Frazer, the only logical explanation for having an Irish flag outside was because it was 'the junior headquarters of SF/IRA youth, or it may as well be … I wonder do they also train the children in how to use weapons, for it seems they can do what they wont.'

We can only hope that junior terrorist cells teach their kids about how to use syntax as well as Semtex.

Of course, there are all sorts of logical reasons why an Irish flag would be flying outside a Tyrone school. Or, indeed, not flying outside a school. Because you see, what Willie Frazer has in sheer pluck and fearlessness he dramatically lacks in vexillology. What he saw wasn't green, white and orange but green, white and red, commonly known as the Italian flag. He also appeared to miss the fact that a Turkish and Polish flag were flying right alongside, but presumably Willie assumed it was some kind of international terrorist gathering, the kind outlined by Alan Rickman in *Die Hard* based on what he read in *TIME* magazine.

Turns out it wasn't a terrorist band camp but an EU cultural exchange project, as 11 teachers from those three countries came to Tyrone to visit. The principal of the school, Dera Calahane, said she was shocked at how 'vindictive and hateful the comments were' and they were taking legal advice and bringing in the PSNI.

Frazer, magnanimous soul that he is, sought to clarify by saying, with his usual Joycean fluidity, 'The flag seen flying at this school is not the Irish tricolour, and it may look very like it but i can asure people it is not.'

Those sneaky Provos may have slipped through that time, but on one issue at least he had the republican menace bang to rights: their interference with the food chain. He claimed, in an interview with the *University Times* that must have had the journalist scooping his hands with glee, that republicans were the ones responsible for all that horsemeat.

When asked why on earth they'd do such a thing, he said, 'To make money. It's the same with cows that have to be sold within a certain number of months after they're born. Basically old fat cows that are 30 months old have been put into the food chain because the republicans have the means of getting it in.'

That all seems pretty logical to me.

❖

Perpetual Embarrassment Rating: 10/10
If Willie finds Italian and Irish flags so confusing, he probably thinks Milan is crawling with Provos.

National Peril-o-meter: 9/10

There's always something very distressing about something so laughable becoming so serious.

'Ah, lads!' Rating: 9/10

'Stuff Willie Frazer Thinks the IRA is Responsible For' is one of the best things on Facebook.

Willie's next plan:

Proving the IRA put figs in the middle of biscuits.

The Time an Election Count Was Stopped by a Poltergeist

Elections in Northern Ireland can be dreary affairs. Because voting is still very much based on how big a deal Jesus' mum was in your early religious education, the results are often fait accompli, so on election days you're looking for something a bit out of the ordinary to spice things up. Thankfully, Northern Ireland is always full of out of the ordinary.

With Sinn Féin and the DUP running so far ahead of the SDLP and UUP they were in danger of being lapped, it fell to Omagh in the 2011 Assembly Election to be the focal point of all electoral mayhem. Even though we all basically knew the order of the parties before a ballot was cast, there was still considerable delay in actually getting them counted. This was partially because of the fact that three counts were going on at once: Assembly, local council and the referendum to introduce the AV system of voting. It was also partially because it seemed a jovial sprite was screwing around with the count in Omagh.

The delays started when a ballot box got rained on, soaking several votes for the Fermanagh/South Tyrone constituency therein. A ballot box that is supposed to be supervised overnight indoors managed to get wet is an enduring mystery. Just as well they weren't electronic voting machines, or there could have been mass electrocutions.

At any rate, the sodden votes were given the hairdryer treatment, literally, as trained vote counters spent their precious hours fanning the votes dry and peeling them off each other. I'd bet you any money somebody also put their tea mug on a couple, leaving a sepia ring on some poor soul's number one vote for Michelle Gildernew.

In another section of the same building the chaos was of a very different kind, as a table collapsed when all the votes were strewn out on it, leaving a mess full of papers and boxes usually reserved for '70s back alley car chases. Given how a table collapsing mid-count is the equivalent of forgetting to save a 2,000-word essay, it's a wonder they managed to keep going at all.

But carry on they did, and eventually, not long before midnight on the count day, the returning officer was in a position to make an announcement. But with it being so late, they were apparently chased out of the actual hall by an angry old janitor or something, and so they did it in the reception area of the community centre. Bizarre as it was to see everyone huddling round him with revolving doors in the background in a foyer like they were queuing up for swimming pool locker keys, everyone was just glad to actually get down to business. But there was to be one more interruption. On live TV, and surrounded by people, the returning officer's phone went off mid-announcement. How embarrassing. His ring tone was Guns 'n' Roses' 'Sweet Child O' Mine'. Ah, good night.

By the following morning – votes dry, tables upstanding and phones set to vibrate – things had settled down somewhat, and with the DUP and Sinn Féin surging into a lead, all seemed pretty normal. But of course this is Northern Ireland, so normal never stays that way for long.

With the live BBC coverage of the election all but winding up to make way for that fixed point in space, *Doctor Who*, the end of the count in Omagh was taking place. It was then that UUP leader Tom Elliott, a man who seems like he knows how to get the best out of a Massey Ferguson and has been 45 since he was 10 years of age, said something that must have made him wish he could turn back the clock. While making his victory speech, Big Tam Elyit couldn't resist making a reference to the Sinn Féin supporters waving tricolours, a common thing among Sinn Féin supporters, in case they forget what nationality they are. 'I see many people here with flags', he said, 'many of them flags of a foreign nation.'

Uh oh.

When sections of the crowd started booing him for the 'foreign' crack, he responded, 'I'd expect nothing more from the scum of Sinn Féin.'

Someone take that man's shovel off him before he hurts himself!

❖

Perpetual Embarrassment Rating: 9/10

It's bad enough the returning officer's phone went off mid-announcement, but a Guns 'n' Roses ringtone?

National Peril-o-meter: 5/10

Tom Elliott and his 'Here, watch this!' Sinn Féin baiting may well have caused ructions, but presumably the Shinners were hoping to get back home in time for *Doctor Who*.

'Ah, lads!' Rating: 8/10

You wait four years for your time to shine as a vote counter, and then rain and dodgy carpentry ruin your shot at the big time. Typical.

Plans to make sure a similar debacle doesn't happen next time:

Votes that can float, to be contained in a hermetically sealed room. Tom Elliott to be sent to similar.

The Time Northern Ireland Spent a Year Celebrating Disasters

If you ask people from Belfast, they will say that for the best part of the twentieth century not much heed or reference was paid to the *Titanic*. Understandable enough, given how more pressing disasters were going on round them for most of that time.

But in 1997, after the four-hours-I'm-never-getting-back of a James Cameron film, Belfast as a city became quite aware that with the whole world going *Titanic* bananas, there might be an avenue to bring some interested parties from around the world to come for the ship, but stay for the ambience. Only in Northern Ireland would you proudly proclaim: 'See that boat that was never supposed to sink but did? Aye, we built that!'

Zoom forward 15 years and the steady build-up to the centenary in 2012. City Hall had museum-style fact boards all over the place, as well as a monument and commemorative garden. A *Titanic* trail was stepped out around the city, and deathly slippery porthole-style looking things were put into the pavements. They really stepped up the commemorative shows on television too, with everything from idents at the beginning of every show to documentaries and dramatisations. In an impressive bit of shoehorning, the BBC even got dance judge Len Goodman, a former Harland & Wolff welder, to do a programme.

But inevitably, it wasn't long before *Titanic* fever reached its convulsive, hallucinogenic peak. The impressive *Titanic* Belfast, that sort of looks a bit like a ship or the most feared boss on Robot Wars, was host to a massive concert run by MTV. Because nothing quite marks a massive maritime disaster like 'Dance with Me Tonight' by Olly Murs.

Titanic Belfast was also host to a massive row over a staircase. A lot was made of their replica staircase which cost £97 million, and with the film still very much fresh in people's memories the public were quite interested to replicate their 'Jack & Rose' moment. Except, it was in the banquet area only available to corporate bookings, and not to the plebs who actually paid for the thing. Things weren't helped when Marvin from JLS and Rochelle from The Saturdays (those troublemakers!) tweeted a picture of themselves on the stairs. The public outcry led Assembly Minister Arlene Foster to intervene to urge the building's powers that be to sort it out, as the whole thing about people being treated differently based on how much money you had or the circles you socialised in was completely distracting from the story of the *Titanic*. Eventually, they relented, and instituted 'Staircase Sundays'. The Belfast Telegraph were there on the first such Staircase Sunday and reported that everyone was very impressed, although one woman noted that the steps looked very small, and wondered 'whether they had smaller feet back then, or whether just because it's a replica'.

But the drive to promote the *Titanic* itself was nothing on companies trying to promote themselves by piggy-backing on the whole boat sink buzz. Tayto released special *Titanic* crisps but Thompson's Tea was possibly the worst offender in opportunism, putting a massive billboard on the Ormeau Road that said, 'Thompson's Puts the T in *Titanic*'. Thankfully, no iceberg companies claimed they 'Put the C in *Titanic*'.

Not to be outdone, though, Northern Ireland's second city had its own bit of ill-fated history they wanted to celebrate. Sinn Féin councillor Elisha McCallion tabled a motion to rename City of Derry Airport to Amelia Earhart, City of Derry Airport, in honour of the legendary aviator who had once landed near where the airport now stands. Except she never intended being there.

Earhart's original intention was to fly from Newfoundland to Paris, but technical trouble and bad weather meant that she was forced to land in Derry, which is quite the silver medal. Choosing to look on the bright side, Councillor McCallion thought it would be a fitting tie-in to the eightieth anniversary of Earhart becoming the first woman to fly solo non-stop across the Atlantic, and there was 'a need to recognise the significant visitor potential the Amelia Earhart legacy holds for the city and district'.

Alas, those killjoys in every other party but Sinn Féin voted against the motion, meaning City of Derry Airport was destined never to be either renamed or have the slogan 'Amelia Earhart Came Here Once by Accident'. But never worry, I'm sure Ulster will have something vaguely unfortunate to commemorate again soon.

❖

Perpetual Embarrassment Rating: 4/10
There's obviously some kind of rule of statute of limitations about what counts as commercial impropriety.

National Peril-o-meter: 2/10
In an odd way, it's probably benefited NI quite well. Even if Marvin and Rochelle were recklessly stirring up trouble.

'Ah, lads!' Rating: 9/10
Some person got paid what I imagine was a lot of money to juxtapose massive billboards, maritime disaster and teabags. Let's all sit and quietly ponder that for a while.

It wouldn't surprise me if:
We hear the creator of the Hindenburg is a Lurgan man.

The Time a Council
Meeting Discussed Eminem

Music and politics are comfortable bedfellows: the work of Elvis Costello, Bono, Billy Bragg and of course Bob Geldof and Midge Ure to give but a few of the obvious examples. But what doesn't go together at all is music and politicians: the awkward shuffling to music of John Prescott and Peter Mandelson at Labour's victory party in 1997, or Boris Yeltsin dancing like a lunatic while trying to get re-elected, for example. And let's not even go anywhere near Donie Cassidy managing T.R. Dallas or Foster & Allen.

And when it comes to concerts and politicians, they often have trouble adjusting to the sick new jams the kids are down with these days. In 1980 Bob Geldof's glorious stubbornness won out over a Dublin court's ruling that The Boomtown Rats would bring untold chaos and societal menace. They held the concert at Leixlip Castle,

Geldof gleefully freaking out the norms and railing against establishment Ireland's fidelity to being shoddy and second rate.

Ambition wasn't so much the problem in Bangor in 2011 but the norms were pretty freaked out as the snarly peroxide-haired Detroit rapper Eminem was due in town. And not just that, but due in town on the same day that the Bangor Missionary Convention, a group not known for its appreciation of the thug life, was celebrating its seventy-fifth anniversary. The late nobel

laureate Seamus Heaney hailed Eminem as a great poet, but the God-fearing and morals-upholding people of Bangor weren't so sure.

'I have no issue with a family-friendly concert in a park …,' claimed pre-eminent nimby Brian Ashworth, '… but this is a performer who uses the crudest language – language that degrades women and has the foulest, most twisted content.'

He didn't just have a problem with Eminem's lyrics, but the noise he'd make while uttering them. 'I have been doing a survey to determine how far the lyrics will be heard and local residents tell me that they heard previous concerts at the park.'

You have to wonder how exactly he conducted that survey, but I can only hope it was with a friend, a megaphone and Brian going 'CAN YOU HEAR ME NOW?', walking back five paces every time.

The matter went to North Down Borough Council, which hadn't actually granted an entertainment licence yet. In spite of the concerns about noise and mortal souls, they duly did by 15 votes to three, as 55,000 tickets were sold and the promoters probably would have sued them if they hadn't. So, while Eminem was Cleaning Out His Closet and going into far too much detail about what happened his Mom's Spaghetti, down the road conventioneers were treated to Isaac Shaw of the Delhi Bible Institute giving 'an inspiring address on his work of training pastors in North India'.

For the following year, though, Bangor's officials weren't so sure about letting it happen again. The Eminem concert that is, the Delhi Bible Institute are welcome back whenever they like, as far as I can gather. Maybe it was because Eminem made the fatal error of shouting 'Hello Belfast!' at the crowd, which caused a dent in civic pride, but I doubt it. North Down Borough Council resolved in March 2012 to only host concerts 'which can only be broadcast on mainstream media', and as far as Deputy Mayor Alan Leslie representing the DUP (sure who else?) was concerned, Eminem wasn't mainstream. 'He would not be my cup of tea ... I did vote against him coming to the town ... because of his foul mouth. And I was right because the council officers have decided not to bring him back again.'

But just to prove he wasn't completely po-faced, he did offer some alternatives: 'If we had something like Country Fest, that would be an idea ... we had Proms in the Park here and that was a great success.'

Country Fest? Jesus, don't tell Donie Cassidy, he'll be calling up his old mates. But Deputy Mayor Leslie did add another blackball to the bag too: 'I would not like to see someone like Rihanna. I think her lyrics are a bit extreme.'

Rihanna, of course, had previous in the Bangor area (see *The Time a DUP Councillor Told Rihanna to Put Them Away*).

The news was met with dismay by the Eminem

fansite TR Shady (the Shady being a reference to his alias Slim Shady, the TR bit presumably suggesting Mr Dallas has more street cred than I realised. Someone get on the phone to Donie!) and by Alliance councillor and young person Michael Bower, who argued that the concert was a good economic stimulant and considered Eminem to be 'moderate'. As if Eminem's extremism was the problem.

❖

Perpetual Embarrassment Rating: 6/10
Eminem, Bangor is like 13 miles away from Belfast. Yeesh.

National Peril-o-meter: 8/10
Not sure what would be more likely to prompt the end of the world as we know it, Jesus making a comeback, or T.R. Dallas.

'Ah, lads!' Rating: 7/10
You get the impression Cliff Richard would be a bit extreme for the good people of Bangor.

Reaction to the Delhi Bible Institute:
Quite positive, I believe.

The Time a Terrorist Got
Caught in a Revolving Door

Northern Ireland's political history is complex, the key figures of that story equally so. Though terrible crimes were committed, everyone involved in the Troubles was someone's son or daughter, they had their own personal hopes and dreams and ambitions, some of them were swept away in crosses to bear, heroes to worship or enemies to demonise, and their circumstances was often more a factor than intrinsic evil.

And of course, some of them were just plain bonkers.

Michael Stone became one of the most notorious faces of loyalism during the Troubles when he attacked the funeral of slain IRA members in Gibraltar with guns and grenades. He started his career (and God knows paramilitarism was about the only growth industry in Northern Ireland at the time) in the early seventies as a member of a 'Tartan Gang', a group of street roughs who maintained their tough demeanour despite looking like the Bay City Rollers. He later joined the UDA and the Red Hand Commando (is it just me or do all these organisations sound like Prog Rock outfits?) and in 1989 was convicted of six murders and sentenced to 684 years in prison. Or as Methuselah would refer to it, 'adolescence'.

He was released as part of the Good Friday Agreement in 2000, getting out of jail 673 years early. He appeared to be a reformed character, endorsing the Good Friday Agreement, meeting with Desmond Tutu and Mo Mowlam and, eh, becoming an artist. *The Telegraph* described his work as 'vivid paintings – lots of bright oranges, reds and purples in a semi-representational style', and one of his pieces sold for £4,000. He claimed David Hockney was an inspiration, 'But he painted pretty boys and something like that wouldn't have gone down too well in the Maze. Some of the inmates on the wing would come up to me and say, "Paint us a nude".'

Not one to spurn the public, Stone duly obliged. 'I stuck a photograph of their girlfriend or wife over the face. It didn't seem to matter whether their woman was like a beanpole or weighed over 25 stone, they seemed to like it.'

The adulation didn't go to his head, though, as when his burgeoning art rep was put to him he said bashfully, 'You're just trying to flatter an old mass murderer.'

Life for Michael Stone seemed quite settled at this point: he had a successful art career in the making, a wife who gave him body armour for Christmas (a better gift than a Lynx set anyway) and a bulletproof aquarium full of tropical fish ('I don't want people to hear that Michael Stone drowned in his own front room because the bullets hit the fish tanks,' was his flawless logic).

But it wasn't enough. He needed more. And so he constructed a daring piece of site-specific art that would truly challenge people. Sort of.

In November 2006, during a crucial setup meeting for the DUP and Sinn Féin to share power together, Michael Stone rocked up to Stormont to perform his work of art. And by 'perform' I mean 'planted pipe bombs around Stormont and tried to enter while in possession of a replica pistol, a garotte, axes, knives and a bomb'. And by 'his work of art', I mean 'tried to kill Gerry Adams and Martin McGuinness'. He was only stopped by that classic counter-terrorism trick: being trapped in revolving doors by security guards.

As Stone was spun out of the revolving doors, arm up his back, he expanded on his 'only performance art' hypothesis by saying he was making a comment on political deadlock to 'put a proverbial rocket up the backsides' of the negotiators. Leaving Cert English students, take note: 'I'm destroying the iconography of Michael Stone, loyalist hero … It's a comic parody of my former self.'

It gets better.

He claimed his outfit on the day was a reference to a

Sunningdale protest he attended in 1974. His fisherman's hat was supposedly a nod to Martin McGuinness' alleged security code nickname 'the fisherman', which must surely go down as the lamest code name ever if true. The sponge inside his replica gun, he said, was an image for 'sponging unionists'. He also had a pair of scissors that represented republicanism, and sported a poppy for 'fallen comrades'. When asked if there would have been any symbolism to his bomb bag going off (it didn't because he got it wet in a rainstorm on the way up to Stormont), he said, 'No, there would not have been.' Pfft, amateur!

The Northern Ireland public, with a gallows humour unrivalled anywhere in the world, reacted to an attempted terrorist storming parliament with 'what is he like?' guffaws.

The Ulster Political Research Group, who have close links to the UDA, said, 'For Michael Stone to act out this gimmick in the most eccentric way was to make our people look petty and irresponsible.'

In court, the judge, philistine that he was, just didn't get Stone's artistic vision and called his justification 'wholly unconvincing' and 'self-contradictory', and sentenced him to 16 years in prison. Everyone's a critic, eh?

❖

Perpetual Embarrassment Rating: 2/10
Michael Stone doesn't do shame!

National Peril-o-meter: 9/10

If they had automatic doors in Stormont, things could have been terrible.

'Ah, lads!' Rating: 9/10

Michael Stone's obviously prepared for court by watching a few episodes of *Boston Legal* or something.

Likely grade in an English exam:

B2. Assuming he didn't try to kill anybody.

The Time Donegal County Council Completely Lost their Gubbins in Front of a Large Group of Teenagers

County councils: the most basic level of democracy. And it doesn't get more basic than in Donegal.

In February 2012, Donegal County Council invited their under-18 counterparts in the Donegal Youth Council to their meeting at the impressive chamber in Lifford. The Youth Council had been running for ten years at this point, over which time young people worked successfully together on matters affecting their schools, their communities and national policy. They did all this with enthusiasm, mutual respect and even temperament.

What a shock it must have been then when they saw a group of adult public representatives have a blazing row in the august chamber in front of them. Four times. Although Donegal County Council had previous on stuff like this, as at one meeting the phrases 'Lose some weight, ya fat bitch!' and 'No wonder your wife divorced you!' were thrown across a room by elected officials.

The first row erupted, as is so often the case, over funding for ferry services. Having had to adjourn the meeting after the minutes stage, it was clear Mayor Noel McBride would have his work cut out keeping order.

Argy number two soon followed, with Fine Gael Councillor John Ryan and Fianna Fáil's Ciaran Brogan having a go at each other like they were in *EastEnders* or something. Cue another adjournment. Small wonder council employees leave at four thirty p.m. with stress like this to deal with.

At this point, it was starting to feel like a full-blown ballroom blitz was about to break out as by-election celebrity Frank McBrearty, a man who knows how to get a party started, took exception to a Sinn Féin press release. To quote the reports of the day, 'Following a second adjournment for five minutes, a fresh round of exchanges broke out, notably between Cllr Frank McBrearty of Labour and Cllr Jack Murray of Sinn Féin, even though the council was not officially conducting business. It is claimed that foul language was used in the chamber.'

Disgraceful. Could they not have waited til the meeting was back on before tearing into each other? Other councillors soon got involved, with Sinn Féin's Marie-Therese Gallagher telling McBrearty to 'take a chill pill'. To be clear, the Donegal Youth Council does not advocate the use of drugs, chill-aiding or otherwise.

Speaking the day after, McBrearty decried what he called Sinn Féin's 'bully boy tactics', but also raised something a bit more worrying: Sinn Féin is some kind of political gorgon. 'Sinn Féin has two faces. They have their face for the public and they have their … their other face that they don't show. I am receiving the abuse from that other face.'

Meanwhile, back in the chamber, Fine Gael's Barry O'Neill was causing quarrel number four, also seeming weirded out/oddly intrigued by Sinn Féin's multiple faces, accusing them of speaking out of both sides of their mouth. Surely that's how everyone does it, otherwise you just look like Clint Eastwood? Anyway, this is when hell truly broke loose. Youth Councillors, who had spent most of the meeting either sinking in their chairs in embarrassment or stifling laughter, then left, as any self-respect the adult councillors had was spent in a widescale row that was only missing swords and people swinging from chandeliers. The hapless Mayor McBride '… appeared to have no control over the proceedings in what was a black day for the council'.

The meeting never got restarted, although Frank McBrearty broke the tension by saying, 'There's ice cream for sale out here – it's the intermission.' If only a choc-ice van had driven by playing 'Greensleeves' earlier in the day, they may have been spared the debacle.

The Donegal Youth Council, bemused and amused in

equal measure, showed the ostensible adults how it's done (prudent governing and diplomacy, that is, not fighting) in the days after following a barrage of media requests asking for quotes on what happened. In the words of one councillor, Ronan Gildea, 'A reporter came looking for a quote from me at school, felt like a hero when I said "no comment".'

Indeed.

❖

Perpetual Embarrassment Rating: 10/10
When it comes to embarrassing scenes, Donegal County Council is the gift that keeps on giving.

National Peril-o-meter: 5/10
Lifford's proximity to the border means that the government could always gently bump the council chamber into Tyrone if things ever got too out of hand.

'Ah, lads!' Rating: 10/10
Won't someone please think of the much more capable and decorous young people?

Possible ideas to stop this happening again:
Reclining red chairs like they have on Graham Norton when someone goes off on one.

Taoiseach's Questionables

The Time Everyone Suspected Brian Cowen Drank the Lakes of Pontchartrain Dry

Granted, there's something about Galway that is all too conducive to staying up partying all night. But when you're the leader of a party and a country, it's probably prudent to spend your nights at a conference maybe sipping a coke and getting to bed before midnight. Especially if you're going to do a tough radio interview the morning after. But this is Brian Cowen we're talking about, a man who thinks that prudence is what you do to trees when they get a bit unruly.

The Fianna Fáil 'think-in' (and I use those quotation marks advisedly) at the Ardilaun Hotel in Galway in September 2010 was supposed to be a chance for the party's great and good to conclave and ponder strategy honestly and without inhibition. And also have a few jars and stay up all night without inhibition.

Brian Cowen held court until three a.m., first doing impressions ('He had us in stitches,' claimed RTÉ's David Davin-Power) and then singing 'The Lakes of Pontchartrain', a performance he announced by saying, 'Whisht up, this is a classic.' Someone no doubt also whispered, 'Oh, he sings this lovely.'

So far, so good for an embattled party leader in need of a shot in the arm popularity-wise, as he was coming under increasing pressure for the perception that he was bumbling, inept and irresponsible. What could possibly go wrong?

For starters, the fact he had an interview on *Morning Ireland* at eight forty-five a.m. Amazingly, it didn't go well. He was far from sharp and very underwhelming in conversation with Cathal Mac Coille, making a series of fluffs like mixing up the Croke Park and Good Friday Agreements and, most noticeably, he sounded like Barry White.

Opposition spokesman Simon Coveney thought that he sounded, more to the point, like Barry White on the black stuff. He tweeted, 'God, what an uninspiring interview by Taoiseach this morning. He sounded half way between drunk and hungover and totally disinterested …'

Reporters, start your microphones.

TV3's Ursula Halligan was the first out of the traps, asking Cowen as he was thronged by journos if he was in fact drunk or hungover. Predictably, Cowen denied it with hurt indignance, but then came the defences from his cabinet underlings. And the excuses. Mary Hanafin and Micheál Martin claimed that he was just hoarse. Dermot Ahern claimed he had nasal congestion, while John Curran gave the kind of excuse that would get a Junior Cert student laughed at and sent to the principal: the Taoiseach just isn't great in the mornings.

Whatever plans Cowen and the government had for that day were trampled like a security guard at an elephant shopping centre during the Boxing Day sales. In the afternoon he gave a press conference decrying all

the hubbub and innuendo about his state on the radio in the morning as 'a new low in Irish politics'. Coveney's tweet, that is, not the interview, or indeed the depth of his voice. Cowen's baritone may not have gone over well to the Irish audience but his voice certainly resonated around the world: within a day of the interview there had been hundreds of articles in dozens of countries, spreading even as far as Qatar and Taiwan. The US was a particular hotbed of reports, playing into the hands of people who still think that Ireland is just like *Darby O'Gill and the Little People* anyway. *Tonight Show* host Jay Leno had a particularly good laugh (unlike any of his audience) as he played a game of 'Bartender, Nightclub Comedian or Irish Prime Minister?' featuring a particularly unflattering detail of Brian Cowen apparently on the lash.

Fianna Fáil's M.J. Nolan wasn't very happy about it, and stated so with the authority only an Oireachtas Committee chairman could muster against an upstart host on one of the longest-running and iconic chat shows on the planet. He said he would have preferred the comment not be made, which really told Leno. He also claimed that the jibe would be seen by international bankers, which could have an effect on Ireland's ability to pay back its many, many debts.

The notion of the Taoiseach not being a morning person and staying up to the wee hours to mimic Micheál Ó Muircheartaigh and belting out ballads about

Louisiana potentially having a similar effect on those international bankers appeared not to feature in M.J. Nolan's thinking.

❖

Perpetual Embarrassment Rating: 10/10
It couldn't have been more embarrassing if he'd gone to the *Morning Ireland* interview with a club stamp on his hand and a tube of Berocca.

National Peril-o-meter: 8/10
When Jay Leno is in a position to make a joke about you, things are not going well.

'Ah, lads!' Rating: 8/10
Up late on a school night, I mean honestly …

Impression I'd most like to hear Brian Cowen do:
Woody Allen.

The Time John Bruton Laid It on with a Shovel for Prince Charles

In fairness, we've all been there. We've all, in the heat or excitement of a moment, over-egged our case a bit when playing it cool was the way to go. This generally happens when approaching a prospective paramour, attending the concert of the flopsy-haired inexplicable heartthrob of the day or, in John Bruton's case, when you're in Dublin Castle at a major diplomatic function.

Fine Gael has long had a reputation for Brit-sympathising and being clean mad about the monarchy and what have you, and in 1995 Taoiseach John Bruton (once referred to as 'John Unionist' in a quality Freudian slip by Albert Reynolds) handed his detractors years' worth of slagging material. He was just supposed to give a toast, but he went a bit overboard on the butter.

Following Big Al Reynolds and Dick Spring's government collapsing in late 1994, John Bruton was basically only Taoiseach for a couple of minutes when

Prince Charles launched over for a visit, the first time a Royal Family member had visited since 1912. This was at a time when we were getting superstar visits from Bill and Hillary Clinton what felt like every fortnight, and also a time when our relationship with Britain was still the kind Taylor Swift would write about. Therefore, an inoffensive, aurally endowed, nice old country rambler like Prince Charles was treated with either indifference or vague suspicion.

Not that you would know that from the fervent reception he got in the rope lines, with one woman in particular being unable to control herself and gripping him in a bearhug-kiss combo, the kind Secret Service agents wake up in the middle of the night screaming about. If you were watching the news that night, you might be forgiven for thinking, 'What an eejit she is, getting so excited about a member of the Royal Family!' Ladies and gentlemen, our Taoiseach.

In a crowded hall of diplomats, distinguished guests and well-dressed habitual party crashers, John Bruton tried his best to come across statesmanlike and magnanimous, but that's not what came out. What came out was described by the British press as 'embarrassingly effusive', with Bruton said to be displaying 'extravagantly nonsensical attitudes'. In fairness, that will happen when you proclaim Prince Charles taking a trip over the sea as 'the happiest day of my life'.

He went on: 'Your presence here, your courage, your

innovation, your initiative in coming here, has done more in symbolic and psychological terms to sweep away the legacy of fear and suspicion that has lain between our two peoples than any other event in my lifetime.'

Jesus.

According to John Bruton, centuries of hostility were parted like the Red Sea by Prince Charles' mighty hand. Also, in praising his innovation, Bruton makes it sound like Prince Charles designed, built and flew his own contraption over the Irish Sea to Dublin Castle. The reality is it's more likely that after hearing a Val Doonican song on his portable garden radio, he went, 'Hmm, Ireland. That'd be nice.'

Hyperbole aside, the meeting was very obviously important for Anglo-Irish relations, and 16 years later Charles' mum showed up, our countries replete by that stage with a Good Friday Agreement and an infinitely more mature attitude. When the Queen addressed Dublin Castle *as Gaeilge*, Mary McAleese only let out an impressed 'Wow.' We've learned so much since the 1990s.

Meanwhile, a few years later, Geri Halliwell would top Bruton in the embarrassing Prince Charles stakes with a toe-curling pastiche of Marilyn Monroe's many happy returns to JFK. The poor man never got a rest.

❖

Perpetual Embarrassment Rating: 9/10
Cringey, yes, but line dancing was very popular at the time too, so in that context we probably shouldn't judge him too harshly.

National Peril-o-meter: 3/10
Although if Charles had caught diabetes from listening to it, I suppose there would have been repercussions.

'Ah, lads!' Rating: 9/10
'Eh, this speech is very good, John, but do you reckon we should keep this bit about how sparkly Prince Charles' eyes are?'

Song used by *Reeling in the Years* when setting this event for posterity:
The Corrs' 'Runaway'. Awww.

The Time Enda Kenny
Wouldn't Attend a Debate

People in this country are clean mad for John Fitzgerald Kennedy. His energy, his vision, the way his visit to the home country genuinely seemed to affect him, his prodigious womanising, everything.

So popular is he in this country that he inspired generation after generation of Irish politicians who are far from liberal icons themselves. Bertie Ahern was forever quoting him, although he always had more of an air of Tammany Hall Boss about him.

But stuffy old Enda Kenny seemed like a less likely fit still. Jack Kennedy was charismatic, progressive, cunning and 100 per cent Massachusetts upper crust. Inda is plain, cautious, a bit gormless and 100 per cent Cashelbar batch loaf. All the same, he's big on JFK, even trying an impression during a TV interview with our pre-eminent

Kennedy scholar, Ryan Tubridy. He was unsuccessful.

But given Kenny's love of JFK you'd think he would have been scrambling to get a replica of Kennedy's finest moments: his debate with Dick Nixon that ended up changing the face of public discourse forever. But Enda wasn't having it.

Granted, there were plenty of them, as Ireland became consumed over the course of the 2011 general election by debate fever. RTÉ had one, TG4 had one, I'm sure if Adam Richman from *Man v. Food* could have got away with a Q&A session/chilli-eating contest he'd have hosted one too. But it was the TV3 one that would prove a debate too far for Kenny. For you see, Enda had a bit of a beef with their moderator.

A couple of months before, the dyspeptic matador of late-night political bullfights Vincent Browne said that Enda Kenny should go into a dark room with a bottle of whiskey and a gun. Vincent apologised the night after but the damage was done. From then on there was a blanket rule from Fine Gael high command: Enda doesn't do Vincent Browne.

Enda's explanation was that Browne's comment was so offensive and insensitive to those who have to cope with suicide that it went beyond the pale, but that only prompted more questions. Why not square up to the man and make a case for better public discourse about mental health, and do it when the whole country would be watching? But, for whatever his reasoning, Enda eschewed the chance to make a game-changing performance, address a massive public policy elephant in the room and

God knows a significant spike in approval ratings if done right. He went to Carrick-on-Shannon instead.

That left Eamon Gilmore and Micheál Martin to their own devices in the TV3 studios with Wee Vinny Crankie. Green Party leader John Gormley, with pathos-drenched opportunism, offered to take Kenny's place, but was politely rebuffed. All in all, given that the rationale for the TV3 debate was supposed to be a clash between the men who would be Taoiseach, the whole thing was utterly pointless since the most likely man to take the post wasn't there. It was like going to see a Destiny's Child concert, except Beyoncé wasn't there. And the other two were replaced by two pasty lads.

Even so, TV3 kept an ember burning for Enda by leaving a chair there for him. Unaffected by that hefty tug on the heart strings, Kenny replied that the empty chair could represent those who had to emigrate. Proof, if it were needed, that he really was making this up as he went along.

Meanwhile, as Martin and Gilmore blathered for well over an hour, a kind of Tantric anti-climax, Enda was in the Bush Hotel giving it socks, and not making trite statements that would warrant someone throwing an empty chair at him. The local press gleefully reported on Kenny's visit: 'Enda Kenny picks Carrick over TV3 debate' boasted the *Leitrim Observer*, and with their patent observing skills also noted, 'Kenny is the only party leader to stop off in County Leitrim so far in the election campaign, other party leaders have visited the two constituencies but failed to hold any event in the county.'

Enda Kenny never made any meaningful attempt to make mental health a policy or debate priority for the duration of the election, more's the pity.

But a year later the issue still wasn't resolved. Maintaining his 'No Browne' rule, he refused to debate with Gerry Adams on the impending fiscal treaty. Vincent even offered to step aside and let Jessica Fletcher/Ursula Halligan hold sway. No dice.

It sort of feels at this point that Enda knows he's been unreasonable, but is too embarrassed to back down. What would JFK say to such refusal to take on a strenuous debate? 'Where all the women at?', probably.

❖

Perpetual Embarrassment Rating: 9/10
An empty chair to represent emigration. I mean, Jesus wept.

National Peril-o-meter: 4/10
But TV3 must have had kittens before their flagship debate all the same.

'Ah, lads!' Rating: 7/10
Can't we all just get along? Oh, right.

Method through which this whole dispute between the two of them should be sorted out:
Gladiator-style pugil sticks.

The Time Bertie
Tried to Flog off Forests

What is it with high-profile Dublin Fianna Fáilers and bloody trees? Ray Burke's shenanigans in west Dublin were bad enough (see *The Time Ray Burke Pulled Up Trees out of Spite*), but then Bertie Ahern, the Freddie Kruger of our national nightmares, supposedly went up every tree in north Dublin looking for Burke's misdeeds. He was obviously looking the wrong way through the binoculars.

Upon leaving office (and a ticking economic time bomb) behind, he set his charges on the International Forestry Fund (IFF), becoming chairman. You'd be forgiven for thinking an organisation with a name like the International Forestry Fund was dedicated to saving the rainforest and giving saplings in poor health nice trips abroad. But Bertie Ahern is involved, remember, so they must be coining it somehow.

Their website says, 'The International Forestry Fund

is a joint venture between Helvetia Wealth AG and IFS Asset Managers Limited.' Ah, there we go. It goes on: 'The International Forestry Fund is a global forestry fund which acquires land for plantation forestry and also acquires existing forests which it manages in a socially responsible manner to achieve a target growth rate of between 5% to 9% per annum.' Growth rate referring to profits as opposed to land used for trees, I imagine. Although, I suppose what better group to deal with forests than a hedge fund?

In 2011, despite being out of office for a few years and ensuring Fianna Fáil would be out of office for many more, he was still suggesting root-and-branch reform of government agencies. Namely, Coillte, the government-sponsored agency that just happens to deal with forests. The IFF released a statement saying, 'Consideration should be given to moving all non-core assets out of Coillte,' barely stifling the impulse to add, 'and then give it to us.'

To back up their suggestion, they made an, eh, uber-slick promotional video that droned on about commercial tropical hardwoods and currency diversification while music more appropriate to a 'We are experiencing technical difficulties' test card played in the background. The kitschy production values were one thing, but at the end Bertie shows up, looking as if he's just come out of the cinema and his eyes haven't adjusted yet. He might not have looked at the top of his game, it may have taken 18 takes to make it look even

that good, but when it came to a breathtaking lack of self-awareness of the words coming out of his mouth, Bertie was impeccable as ever. 'I believe we all have a duty to act in a socially responsible manner, in our lives and also in the manner in which we invest,' he said, with no irony or shame whatsoever.

Further enhancing his Ron Burgundy-esque ability to read whatever is in front of him, he too talked a bit about diversificationy, per annum profit marginy, syngerisingy gubbins, before assuring their forestries were run responsibly in accordance with best forestry principles. What he knows about forestry, responsibility or principles is anyone's guess.

Bertie's shameless pursuit of high-paying retirement adventures isn't restricted to a stroll in the woods, though; he was for a while to be found regularly on the hill. Capitol Hill, specifically.

For reasons that couldn't be figured out with a high-powered calculator and a Rosetta stone, the Washington Speakers Bureau had him on their roster of speakers, being paid €30,000 a pop to, ya know, slabber on a bit.

The Bureau, which braves the slogan 'Connecting you with the world's finest minds' and apart from former heads of state boasts other speaker categories like 'Top Executives', 'Heroes' and, eh, 'Gymnasts', had Ahern as one of their premium speakers, his bio at the time saying:

> *During his tenure as prime minister, Ahern transformed Ireland from one of the poorest countries in the world to one of the wealthiest. A period of economic prosperity called the 'Celtic Tiger' led to an unprecedented rise in disposable income. Unemployment fell from 18 percent to 3.5 percent, and the average industrial wage grew to one of the highest in Europe. Public debt was dramatically reduced while Ahern oversaw large investments in the modernization of cities and infrastructure.*

Groucho Marx couldn't have done better.

Alas for him, and the various audiences denied his wisdom, the Bureau dropped him in 2012 around the time of the Mahon Tribunal findings, which were so bad even Fianna Fáil moved to expel him. They then dropped the bio, for crimes against hubris. But before he was taken off the very expensive rubber chicken circuit he did get an invitation that became notorious: speaking at an economic conference in the political corruption haven of Nigeria. Being a country full of suspiciously wealthy princes, Bertie was no doubt in his element.

Apparently he was 'well received' for an 'inspirational speech', with one source telling the *Irish Independent*: 'He is seen as an inspiration over there. He already advises the Nigerian government on economic issues [!] but this event was separate. We have a saying – "A prophet is not without honour, save in his own country."'

I think ye misspelt 'profit' there, lads.

Of course, Bertie Ahern's quest for filthy lucre doesn't end there. Not only is he willing to stand at Nigerian lecterns for money, but he's also willing to sit in advertising kitchen fittings for money. Yup, he even took the Murdoch shilling, writing sports articles for the *News of the World* – a paper that was shut down for being just awful – appearing in a television ad having a cup of tea. In a cupboard. And then consider the money he was getting from the time he sat in the other cabinet, where to this day he picks up a yearly pension of €150,000, despite saying he would give a portion of it back to the State.

But that's Bertie, he doesn't just want to feather his nest, he wants the tree it's in too.

❖

Perpetual Embarrassment Rating· 10/10
Bertie? Embarrassment? He has as much shame as a wealthy Nigerian prince has willing replies to his email.

National Peril-o-meter: 10/10
Not happy to let the country go up in flames, he tries to take our kindling too.

'Ah, lads!' Rating: 8/10
How can a Swiss wealth fund have production values so bad for a promotional video?

Substance Bertie's neck is made out of:
Hard to say, but if they made a chainsaw out of it, it could probably cut through a giant redwood in seconds.

The Time Enda Told
Us It Wasn't Our Fault

When a Taoiseach stares at you down the camera, you know things are a hames. Jack Lynch did it in 1969 when things looked so dire in Northern Ireland that the border was going to melt off. Charles Haughey did it in 1980 when he told us as a community we were living way beyond our means. So bad was the economic situation then that even if he sold all the brass in his neck at an impressive mark-up, we'd still be in arrears.

And so it fell to Enda Kenny, carousel master in our latest wheel o'calamity, to address the nation before his government's first ever budget. It was going to be a landmark event, so it was important he not resort to cliché too early.

A few lines in he said, 'We live in exceptional times.'

Jesus, here we go.

He carried on, and if you had just come in from

the kitchen to hear 'I would love to tell you that our economic problems are solved, that the worst is over', you may have done a V-J Day-style whoop and holler, but the mood was brought right down when he immediately added, 'But for far too many of you, that is simply not the truth.'

Oh.

In case you weren't feeling bad enough, he then got into the specific kind of misery people were experiencing: 'You may be looking at your adult children. Wondering how you'll say goodbye to some of them as they leave Ireland in search of new opportunity in the New Year.'

If any buzz was still alive at this point, Enda punched it in the face. Although, mind you, the pain of saying goodbye to your adult children is probably slightly better than wondering when the hell your adult children will be able to move out and afford somewhere else.

After throwing a Radiohead album worth of depression our way, he then wound up for the line that would become the hinge of the whole speech: 'Let me say this to you all: You are not responsible for the crisis.'

Which must have relieved Michael Fingleton, sitting at home watching in his underpants and stupid hat eating Doritos.

While it was nice of Enda to say so, the spirit of it was rather negated by the fact that he then outlined the specific ways in which we'd be punished anyway. 'In this Budget we must cut public spending by €2.2 billion and raise €1.6 billion in extra taxes … This budget will be tough – it has to be. It will move us towards a manageable deficit of 3 per cent of our GDP by 2015.'

Although nothing quite consoles the nation like manageable economic data extrapolation, he did try and bolster his empathy bona fides with that obligatory old political speech trope: referencing an actual human.

'I get to meet lots of people in this job – a woman in Limerick whose husband had found work after being on the live register for months told me he did not just get back his job, he got back his dignity; once more he felt he was making a contribution.'

Again, lovely anecdote, but within a couple of minutes he was talking about just how big a contribution that man in Limerick and everyone else would have to make. 'To give you some certainty for the year ahead, we're leaving income tax untouched. Instead, we will raise the €1.6 billion of extra taxes that Ireland needs mainly through indirect taxes, difficult though these will be.'

Brilliant: they won't kick the door down, but they will climb in through the window.

Coming to the end of the speech and in need of a rousing point, Enda seemed to momentarily think he was singing at the end of *Les Misérables*, with a sequence of lines that wouldn't have felt out of place as motivational posters in a Stalinist office block. 'Towards more jobs. Towards more opportunities. Towards renewed confidence.'

He finished off as any sensible Irish politician in trouble would, harking back to the Free State founders. 'Next Tuesday, December 6th, is the ninetieth anniversary of the signing of the Treaty in 1921. Just as our fledgling State made its way to becoming a Republic then – I believe with all my heart that we the Irish people can now make our way to recovery.'

Not a bad ending, but the line he drew could have been better, given how that fledgling Free State took 27 years to become a Republic.

Reaction was, inevitably, immediate. A Twitter hashtag mischievously titled #stateofenda was awash with jokes about how he should have signed off in German and whatnot, but the plus points were more or less restricted to 'Well at least he talked to us.'

Gerry Adams called the speech a wasted opportunity for a route to growth, but as he wasn't on Twitter at the time (see *The Time Gerry Adams Wrote a Twitter Stream of Consciousness*) neglected to tell us what his dog or teddies thought of it.

Fianna Fáil released a statement saying Kenny had said nothing new, a statement to that effect itself being nothing new. PR woman Terry Prone, who seems to have set up a magic circle for herself in getting paid to coach politicians in how to present themselves properly, and then get paid to go on panel shows and discuss how well they did, said that the likes of Roosevelt had an advantage over Kenny when it came to talking to the nation. No kidding. FDR had 'The only thing we have to fear is fear itself.' Enda had '50 quangos will be abolished or merged.'

But the best reaction goes to the person on Twitter who pledged they'd never vote Fine Gael again, because the address had delayed the start of *Love/Hate* by ten minutes. Enda would be getting plenty of the latter after his ill-fated trip to Davos.

The Time Enda Told
Other People It Sort Of Was

The whole concept of the Davos Economic Forum seems like it was based on a speculative phone call to event planners by an indecisive account handler. 'Hello, I'd like to organise an international conference about economics in an ostentatiously salubrious background with a hint of Bond villain headquarters about it. Davos, you say? Sounds wonderful!'

Davos has become a focal point for the great, good and garish for quite a while now, and with Ireland's recent economic notoriety Enda Kenny was going to be in their line of sight eventually. In 2012, mere weeks after his Address to the Nation, he was one of the speakers at a part of the conference called Rebuilding Europe, a mid-ticket item in the schedule. But, as many's a smug music festival fan will tell you, you always have a good chance of seeing something quite remarkable down ticket that will eventually become huge. This was one such event. Along with Kenny were the Finnish PM Jyrki Katainen, Polish president Bronisław Komorowski and Danish statsminister and real-life Birgitte Nyborg, Helle Thorning-Schmidt. In fairness to Enda, if I was sitting beside Helle Thorning-Schmidt I'd have probably lost the run of myself too, but whether it was that or the Swiss mountain air going for him, he released an extraordinary hostage to fortune.

While explaining the Irish situation to the not-quite packed audience, he said, 'What happened in our country is that people simply went mad with borrowing.' He said some stuff after that, but really, after a line like that, who cares?

The reaction was inevitably one of howling dismay. Surrounded by other EU leaders and associated high rollers, he seemed to be strumming a different tune to that he gave the Irish hoi polloi on the telly not long before, a lot more 'We all partied' than 'You are not to blame'. It was also, incidentally, a lot different to his comments after the Fine Gael Árd Fheis in 2007, when he said that he didn't foresee any change in economic circumstances given the ESRI's outlook on the situation.

So with the apparent zealot of the convert, Kenny raised the ire of the Opposition, and the public. Pádraig Mac Lochlainn of Sinn Féin called it 'an appallingly ignorant synopsis of the crisis', while one commenter on TheJournal.ie scoffed at his gleeful body language among his peers and simultaneous portrayal of the Irish public as 'the big thickos on the island'.

The timing of the comments weren't just bad because they came so close to the budget, but because just a week earlier Michael Noonan had characterised emigration as 'a lifestyle choice', ignoring the fact that a lot of people were doing so because they had no chance of a lifestyle back home. But if the Irish people weren't wild about their performance, the people at Davos had no such qualms, as Kenny and Noonan were invited to open the European markets in 2013, and they got to hit a big gong to boot. A big gong! If ever there was a sign of recovery …

❖

Perpetual Embarrassment Rating: 8/10
Seeing Enda puff out the chest in front of his European peers was ever so slightly nails on a chalkboard.

National Peril-o-meter: 7/10
It seems that anything you say abroad can be heard back home these days, so you need to be careful. Internet, eh?

'Ah, lads!' Rating: 8/10
It's amazing what the Danish PM and the promise of a big gong can do to a man's judgement.

Hot chocolate on the après-ski at Davos:
I bet it's terrific.

The Time Enda
Appeared in *Time*

There are certain things in life that indicate that you've made it, and getting your nyuk on the cover of *Time* magazine ranks up there, along with winning a Nobel Prize, an Oscar, or hosting *The Late Late Show*. But in October 2012, unassuming old Enda Kenny took his place in the canon of the world's most illustrious cover page, like Hitler, Nixon and a three-year-old being graphically breastfed by his mum.

The piece was titled 'The Celtic Comeback' (rejected titles include 'Ireland: Nothing To See Here') and both that and the *Time* logo were replete in green. They obviously figured having a leprechaun on Kenny's shoulder might be a little on the nose, and also because they had done that exact thing when Seán Lemass made the cover many years previously.

There was, inevitably yet lamentably, a fair bit of

toorah loorah malarkey woven into the piece. One of the sections was titled 'Oh Kenny Boy', for example, and in a quote referring to Kenny's clear love of the political cut and thrust, interviewer Catherine Meyer (who, in a Russian matryoshka doll type setup, was then interviewed about the interview by Sorcha Pollak) opined, 'He seems less like a man in it for the glory than the craic', before leaving us with her final salvo: 'The luck of the Irish may be that Kenny stepped forward.'

Gawd.

The fact that Kenny seems to be better regarded on the international stage while people back home are bemused at what the fuss is about – a kind of political alternative to the *Mrs Brown's Boys* phenomenon – comes up regularly in the piece.

'At 61, Kenny appears every inch the alpha politician, with hair as thick as Mitt Romney's, an avuncular twinkle and a face equally suited to the somber and the celebratory. People trust him.'

But political strength and alphadom on the world stage isn't just marked by hair thickness, or a versatile face. Apparently the ability to climb a mountain will do it too: 'Politicians rarely endure as long as Kenny, or attain high office, without a palette of skills, sensitive antennae and an iron constitution. Kenny's enduring good humor and busy schedule indicate stamina; his 2003 ascent of Mount Kilimanjaro attests to physical endurance.'

Apart from apparently being in the pantheon of

political greats, he also has a bit of a celeb cache. 'He loves The Boss,' explains Meyer. Bruce Springsteen that is, not Haughey. Or Merkel. He was also compared to Peter Sellers' character Chauncey for his capacity to say very simple things mistaken for profundity ('If you have a good base of a thriving economy where people have the opportunity to do what it is they can do, which is be creative and different and helping others, that's the kind of Ireland that we like'). But at least he avoided Clouseau.

For all his well-regardedness on the international stage, his domestic status as well as the delicate subject of his being at the helm of a rust-bucket economy had to be addressed eventually. On the topic of taking the hard decisions, he said, 'I've no interest in looking for either credit or thanks,' which is just as well I suppose.

But as you might expect, he put a brave face on things. He made a virtue of Ireland's 'tax flexibility', i.e. bending over backwards to make sure multinational companies don't have to pay a whole pile. He also boasted that Ireland has 'the best demographics in Europe', which also happens to be our best export. One line that must have caused Enda worry was a quote from Mario Draghi that praised him as 'a model of compliance'. Draghi may as well have dropped Enda to work right outside the Dáil gates in a pink dressing gown and carpet slippers.

Draghi wasn't the only person to offer a quote to the

piece, though. Previous Fine Gael leader and Taoiseach by default John Bruton did too, a quote that arguably revealed more about him than about Kenny. 'He's a person it's not really possible to dislike, and that's very important. It's a quality that not all of us have,' says Bruton, the last Fine Gael Taoiseach, ruefully. 'It's really good for the country that we have someone like that at this particularly difficult moment in the job of Taoiseach.'

But while Bruton might think it's important to have an austerity leader who doesn't have a very punchable face, the reaction proved that quite a few had no particular problems, if not disliking him, then taking the mick. Photoshopped versions of the cover started to spring up, things like '*Time* ... to emigrate' or Enda with The Joker makeup on. The most intricate one though goes to the person who superimposed the head of Podge (or is it Rodge?) on the cover, with the explanatory note suggesting the article was 'In the hope that some yank investor will drink one too many, start up shop over here, and wake up with the greatest hangover of all fucking time'. I would not be surprised if that was actually written on a *Time* magazine ideas flipchart.

Elsewhere, the universally loved music-itarian and financial Dutchman Bono claimed that *Time* got it wrong, and agreed with a sentiment he attributed to Kenny that they should have had the Irish people on the cover. That probably would have made for a bit of a space issue, although at the rate people have poured out of the country, maybe not. Mattie McGrath also made a comment on the article, but he confused *Time* with *Playboy*. Now that would have been a terrifying exposé.

❖

Perpetual Embarrassment Rating: 3/10
All in all it's not a bad thing to see the head of government on an international magazine. And he didn't quote Darby O'Gill once.

National Peril-o-meter: 2/10
We were pretty much in the clear once the title of the piece wasn't 'GET OUT WHILE YOU STILL CAN'.

'Ah, lads!' Rating: 7/10
'Oh Kenny Boy', seriously like. At least they didn't mention Flatley.

Number of times Enda has gone into different newsagents buying multiple copies while wearing a moustache:
Several.

The Epics

The Time We Gave a Guarantee and Made Everything Uncertain Forever, Part 1

It's over half a decade since that TV ad woman got up in the middle of a bus and made that immortal confession, 'I don't know what a tracker mortgage is.' Turns out nobody, not least the people selling them, had much of a clue either.

The notorious Anglo Tapes bear this out, providing proof if it was needed that Ireland's banking elite were a disgustingly inept cross between Watergate conspirators and the guys from that Budweiser 'WAZZUP!' ad. John Bowe picking €7 billion out of his arse as the cost of Anglo's bailout and singing the German national anthem. Their generally stunning gamesmanship in dealing with the whole country's financial health. It's a compelling case to reintroduce stocks and free public arse kickings.

But it's not like the authorities did much to stop them.

Ireland's descent into the seventh circle of economic hell certainly wasn't foreseen by Bertie Ahern, who back in 2007 responding to 'cribbers and moaners' talking down the economy, gave probably the single most appalling statement in modern Irish politics: 'I don't know how people who engage in that don't commit suicide.'

The coyote of international finance finally plummeted in 2008, once it looked down and realised it had nothing but sky under its feet and had run out of cliff a long, long time ago. In the States, Fannie Mae, Freddie Mac,

Bear Stearns and Lehman Brothers all held a sign saying 'Yikes!', while in the UK it was Northern Rock that came off worst.

With a run on the bank not seen since George Bailey forsook his honeymoon in *It's A Wonderful Life*, the idea of bank guarantees started coming to the fore. Finance Minister Brian Lenihan, a barrister whose experience with numbers prior to becoming the nation's foremost money man was a few light games of *Countdown*, floated the idea of a wholesale guarantee for Ireland's banks, and unilaterally went for it. Europe paternally responded: '… the ECB notes that the Irish authorities have opted for an individual response to the current financial situation and not sought to consult their EU partners. In view of the similarities of the causes and consequences of the current financial distress across EU Member States and the potential interdependencies of policy responses, it would have been advisable to properly consult other EU authorities on the envisaged legislative plans.'

With consultation being for wimps, Brian Lenihan boasted that it would be 'the cheapest bailout in the world', at a mere €440 billion for six banks. I mean, that's only like … €70-something billion per bank! RTÉ ran the buoyant headline 'Banking guarantee bolsters Irish government' in the immediate aftermath, and the government's charitable '*Mi debt es su debt*' proposal may have been a genuine attempt to stop people extracting

ATMs from the wall after they refused them money. But it seemed to overlook one crucial thing: the banks. In fact, they overlooked them for 15 years, which was sort of the problem.

What happened next is all too well known. The government flailed around like a person who had knocked over an invaluable china set in a house they were supposed to be minding, while those free market titans found that socialism wasn't all that bad when it was applied to them, and boy was it applied. A few billion here for Anglo, a few billion there for Bank of Ireland and Allied Irish, and nationalisation everywhere.

The Time We Gave a Guarantee and Made Everything Uncertain Forever, Part 2

You'd think their dramatic fall from grace cushioned only by the taxpayer would have chastened some of the big hitters, but not so. Anglo's Seanie FitzPatrick called on the government to tackle the 'sacred cows' of universal child benefit and State pensions. He also railed against what he called excessive regulation of Irish banks and said of the crisis, 'The cause of our problem was global, so I can't say "sorry" with any kind of sincerity.'

You'd wonder what he could say with any kind of sincerity.

Michael Soden, former chief at Bank of Ireland and Central Bank advisor, weighed in too with some intriguing suggestions. After criticising the EU and questioning whether we compromised our sovereignty by joining, he then stated the case for, eh, becoming the fifty-first state of the USA. 'The possible consequences of political and economic association with the US would be a massive influx of foreign direct investment, a link to the US dollar, a reduction in unemployment, and who knows, maybe an annual payment for a number of years to get our finances back in balance.'

Surely it's not foreign direct investment any more if you actually join the country?

Before you wonder too much about the parallel logic dimension he seems to have found, though, it's worth saying that this is the same Michael Soden who resigned from the Bank of Ireland over looking at nudey pictures on his work computer.

Ivan Yates was hardly a financial big shot miscreant, but he too, along with the likes of Colm McCarthy's Bord Snip Nua proposals, held a blistering 'Dig up, Stupid' line on Ireland's monetary woes, the new vogue notion being that Ireland's main problems were in its government spending. This seemed to work off the basis that the billions and billions used to mollify the increasingly crack-addled banks was so high only dogs could hear it, but the €966 million on non means-tested free schemes, as he outlined in his *Irish Examiner* column in October 2010, was intolerable.

Yates echoed Ireland's favourite effigy FitzPatrick by imploring us to 'slaughter some sacred cows' and 'let's get off all those freebies'. He even laid his deficit hawk talons into the Defence Forces on his Newstalk show at one point, asking a (very well-briefed) army officer was there any real need for it. The officer gave him a very well-polished boot up his argument. The arch-troubleshooter Yates would later give up the column and the radio show to concentrate on his own financial affairs, as months after his sacred cows article his bookies went into receivership.

Apple merchant and 'salt a' de eart' businessman Bill Cullen also chipped in his two cents about what was wrong with society. He went on RTÉ's *The Frontline* to blast a molly-coddled, indolent youth that expect the government to pick up after them and are unwilling to go out and make their own opportunities. That from a man best known for a car dealership that benefited greatly from a government-sponsored scrappage deal, and a TV show that was based on an idea that was based on an idea from another guy. In 2012, his business Glencullen Holdings was put into receivership. Can you see a pattern emerging?

Public arrogance and personal money woes were far from the sole preserve of the private sector, though, as the State's tap-dancing on quicksand was going to need a bailout. Not that anybody in government was prepared to say that, with the most common phrase coming from Government Buildings being that we were 'fully funded into the middle of next year'. They phrased it that way because presumably 'We are totally running out of money, but just not quite yet' was a little bit on the nose.

The canary in the mineshaft though was Dermot

Ahern, or rather the canary was tied in a Windsor knot around his neck, as he went on *The Week in Politics* wearing a much-talked-about yellow tie calling bailout speculation 'fiction'. 'We have not applied, there are no negotiations going on. If there were, government would obviously be aware of it and we are not aware of it,' claimed the Minister for Justice.

'Ireland formally asks for EU help' was the RTÉ headline within days.

It was at that point that Ireland's knowledge of Indian economists and Russian loanwords went through the roof, as you could barely move for hearing 'A.J. Chopra' or 'Troika' for the next, oh, forever. News of Ireland's chastened economic woe was of course world news, with sympathetic reports in Latvia and Georgia. When countries that endured Soviet nonsense for decades feel sorry for you, you know things have gone slightly awry.

Several years and an incalculable number of column inches later, economic confusion still looms large. In April 2013 Ashoka Mody, an architect of the IMF's bailout plan, admitted mistakes were made and that 'reliance on austerity was counterproductive'. A month later a Brussels-based think tank claimed that Ireland's bailout had been a success. And a few weeks after that came the Anglo Tapes.

To quote the philosopher Patrick McCusker, 'The problem with unregulated banking is you eventually run out of other people's money.'

❖

Perpetual Embarrassment Rating: 10/10

'Oh, we totally have enough money, believe me … but just to be on the safe side …'

National Peril-o-meter: 10/10

Eh …

'Ah, lads!' Rating: 10/10

Has the world ever encountered a bigger band of douche bags than the Anglo Tapes crew?

Idea for a dramatisation of the crisis:

An economic allegory set in the Wild West called *He Wore A Yellow Tie*.

The Time a Whole Pile of People Wanted to Live in the Zoo, Part 1

The Irish presidency has undergone an overhaul in recent times. When at one stage it was essentially the political equivalent of being given a nice pen at a retirement party (a Fianna Fáil retirement party at that), ever since the blessed Mary Robinson took office in 1990 it's meant a lot more. The head of government oversees the body politic, but the head of state is the soul of the nation. The Taoiseach browbeats us and has to force us to eat our greens, but the President indulges us with a trip to the ice cream parlour and tells us how great we are.

Mary Robinson, with her dedication to solving world wrongs, her devotion to the diaspora and her formidable legal mind and liberalism, was that rarest of Irish statespeople: a person on the world stage who wouldn't comprehensively embarrass the arses off us.

She was succeeded by Mary McAleese, who with characteristic cleverness pledged to carry on the track pioneered by Robinson without raking over the one left by the past Fianna Fáil incumbents. But after Mary's 14 years of building bridges, it was time in 2011 for a new course. It's a bit like getting a new Doctor Who but instead of a short, mysterious burst of regenerative energy, the process takes ages and leaves every single detail of the candidates' lives out in the open for anyone to have a poke at.

First candidate out the gate could easily have been a Timelord, Senator David Norris. The Joycean scholar with an air of Toad Hall bounded into an early lead before most others had even put their name in the ring, and his status as a gay Anglican eccentric national treasure rights advocate marked him out as a classic candidate for an increasingly atypical office. In addition, as a man who was credited with single-handedly overturning the law that made Wilde a criminal and also single-handedly rehabilitating the reputation of James Joyce, his hands secmed as fearsome as Bruce Lee's.

Despite his supremacy in the early stages of the race, other candidates also fancied a shot at the Áras. Mary Davis, the organiser of the wildly successful Special Olympics in Ireland in 2003, thought that and other such experiences in the NGO sector would be enough to make her the third Mary on the trot in the big seat.

Gay Mitchell, Fine Gael's answer to the question

'What if Mr Bean was from Inchicore?', also threw his hat in the ring, fighting off competition at the primary stage from wellies-on-camera-wearer-turned-MEP Mairead McGuinness and self-licking lollipop Pat Cox, former European Parliament President and the sort of man who'd make a cracking cameo in *Ally McBeal* as a flamboyant trial lawyer. Cox ran for the nomination despite the fact he had only been a member of the party for three days, yet was still the favoured candidate of the FG leadership. This was because he had impressive contacts on the international political circuit, and also because he was a Teflon pan to Gay Mitchell's wire scouring brush.

At the Fine Gael convention, abrasion won, much to Enda Kenny's discomfort. So much so, in fact, that he snipped at a journalist, 'Am I supposed to be going around grinning like a Cheshire Cat at everything?'

Things over at Labour were more clear cut, as Michael D. Higgins finally got a shot at the presidency, his name being thrown around as a candidate since before Mary Robinson got the gig. He was joined by a woman who tried to succeed Mary in 1997, Dana Rosemary Scallon, which is fitting because her platform was essentially an attempt to turn the clock back a decade and a half at least. She was in the middle of managing a team on RTÉ's *Celebrity Bainisteoir* when she announced she would run, the first (and I'm guessing will be the only) instance in the world of someone dropping out of a TV sports programme to run for high office. She was joined by fellow Derry dweller Martin McGuinness, representing Sinn Féin in their first presidential bid, with a view to being in the big house for the Easter Rising centenary. The sprawling field was fenced in by Sean Gallagher, the follicly challenged star of *Dragons' Den*, and thus a man who could credibly have put his pinkie to his mouth and shouted ONE MILLION DOLLARS! at some point in his career. But there was one notable absence: a Fianna Fáil party candidate.

Yup, despite having handpicked every president bar

one since the end of the Second World War, Fianna Fáil were so traumatised by their wet fish beating in the general election earlier that year (see *The Time Fianna Fáil Exploded*) they decided against putting forward a candidate, despite the likes of Brian Crowley and Éamon Ó Cuív expressing a masochistic wish to run.

And so, seven fine candidates of virtue true took to their Socratic podia in a bid to win the most dignified political office in the land.

And by that I mean they beat the lining out of each other.

The Time a Whole Pile of People Wanted to Live in the Zoo, Part 2

Never have so many candidates been put through so much for so little actual hard power as the presidential election in 2011. Long-term front runner David Norris was the first to crash out, a gentleman racer in the political demolition derby. Despite his popularity with the public, due to rules of becoming a candidate resembling that of a Japanese game show, he found getting 20 Oireachtas members or four county or city councils to back him surprisingly hard. The most ludicrous instance happened at Galway City Council, who refused to even give him a hearing. Although they had a perfectly good excuse: Council Mayor Hildegarde Naughton thought she was voting against endorsing Norris, not just giving him a hearing, and got confused. Jesus.

He made a serious lapse of judgement however when he wrote a letter appealing for clemency for his old friend and lover Ezra Nawi, convicted in Israel for having sex with a 15-year-old. The letter was on headed paper, he mentioned his future presidential hopes, campaign staff resigned, TDs withdrew their support, and that was the end of that.

With Norris' big personality out of the race, a vacuum needed to be filled, and so began a series of draft campaigns for candidates, most of whose sole qualification was being able to stand in front of a mic without bursting into tears. Gay Byrne was first, but the idea fizzled out around the time he exclaimed, 'Ireland is run by mad people in Brussels.' Miriam O'Callaghan was next, but she dodged it out of hand. Then Micheál Ó Muircheartaigh was floated, and in spite of being very interested (and probably impossible to vote against), it never went any further than the consultation stage. And then, possibly the best suggestion of all cropped up: Martin Sheen.

Thousands of box-set-owning Bartlet lovers online thought the idea of the *West Wing* President transferring over to the old country to be an irresistible proposition, as did the news outlets worldwide who gleefully covered it. In fact the only man to resist was Martin Sheen himself who, while flattered, said he was 'simply not qualified', which didn't seem to stop most of the other candidates.

Meanwhile at Fine Gael HQ, Gay Mitchell wasn't put off by the fact that a fictional former Governor of New Hampshire was much more popular than he was, or his

The CANDIDATES STAND on THEIR RECORDS....

WHATEVER....WE WILL STILL GET AN EX-STAUNCH FIANNA FAIL PRESIDENT FOR AN EX-STAUNCH FIANNA FAIL PEOPLE...

reputation of being able to start a quarrel in a cloister full of nuns on a vow of silence. He caused much opprobrium after saying he would 'jump off O'Connell Bridge' if anyone told him to smile more again. Organisations that deal with suicide prevention took their glasses off and pinched their nose, but Mitchell explained that 'smiles do not deliver jobs, smiles do not deliver the sort of thing that this country needs, which is moral leadership'. Gay Mitchell: fun-loving guy.

He also boasted two different sets of posters, one of him looking into the future while a busy street zooms by him, the inexplicable other featuring him in a wax jacket with a tractor behind him, in case the rural voters found roads and pedestrians a bit intimidating.

His party didn't do him many favours either mind, as they thought going comically negative on Sinn Féin was a world-beating strategy. Phil Hogan claimed American corporate types, hot house flowers that they are, would be appalled – appalled! – that an ex-'RA man could be head of state, seemingly unaware that McGuinness was invited to ring the Wall Street bell the year before. Chief Whip Ian Kehoe nearly lost his job after he tweeted, in response to McGuinness' pledge to take the average industrial wage, that he'd be well able since he still had a bit of that Northern Bank robbery money floating about.

Fine Gael's reaction to Martin McGuinness was indicative of McG's campaign, though: marked by references to his paramilitary past. At one point, it seemed every time he went on the canvass someone who lost family members at the hands of the IRA took him to task about his involvement. It all came to a head under the hot lights of the TV debate studios when Vincent Browne pulled out a series of books, 'Subterranean Homesick Blues' style, that claim he was still in the IRA well after he claimed he wasn't. The pendulum swung his way though after Miriam O'Callaghan furnished us with the second best eye-rub-of-disbelief moment of the whole campaign (more on that anon) by asking McGuinness how he reconciled his Catholicism with giving the go-orders for murder. That, plus hilariously overblown post-event coverage in the newspapers ('The IRA godfather went into a hissy fit at the RTÉ studios and tried to intimidate the mother-of-eight', reported *The Herald*), swung sympathy his way. He even developed a habit for saying some very interesting things, like pledging to open the Áras to the poor on Christmas Day, and endorsing celebrations of the Ulster Solemn League and Covenant. Dana, however, had neither sympathy nor interesting things to say.

During that same Miriam-Martin-Murder-Mesh debate she went off-piste, from waving around a copy of the Constitution to making a dramatic statement. She hit out at allegations about to be made against a member of her family she called 'malicious and vile', claiming they were being used to 'destroy my good character'. Nobody had a clue what the hell she was on about.

Despite Miriam's attempts to tease it out of her, Dana left it hanging there like an interminable drum roll, announcing something she had no intention of elaborating on. People might have taken the suggestions more seriously if she hadn't already been crying wolf earlier in the campaign. At one stage on the campaign trail she claimed dirty tricks when her tyre blew on the motorway, leading her to think someone had tampered with it. I always knew Dana lived in the 1950s, I just didn't realise she lived in a 1950s Hitchcock film. Just as well the campaign didn't last any longer, or a crop duster plane may have come after her while she was canvassing in the countryside.

The Time a Whole Pile of People Wanted to Live in the Zoo, Part 3: The Final Insult

With mud being flung everywhere during the election, it was thought studio lights would be the best detergent. Candidates underwent approximately three zillion debates, give or take a zillion. But one of the most telling debates of the whole campaign wasn't on TV or radio, but streamed online from an old lecture hall in UCD.

Hosted by SpunOut.ie, five of the seven candidates (Dana begged off, while Mitchell had people to alienate in Cork that day) faced a star chamber of young people in their teens and twenties, and facing their ire in particular was Mary Davis, who had become less connected with the Special Olympics and much more associated with Special K. Her glossy posters featuring her catwalking in a fuchsia-pink dress appeared to be photoshopped to kingdom come and one of the audience, Rachael McNulty, asked her whether photoshopping her posters was a good idea or good example, given how so many young girls are concerned with body image. The crowd erupted. Mary insisted they weren't, the crowd erupted again. Checkmate.

One candidate who had no such problems was Michael D. Higgins. His popularity was borne out in the variation on a theme to his 'President with Purpose' posters, featuring a beaming Higgins with hands out wide in an 'Ah it's yourself!' pose. Higgins was photoshopped harnessing a magic orb with the tagline 'The President Who Is a Wizard'. At the SpunOut debate, he won the crowd over with a rollicking speech that has since become known as 'Be the Arrow, Not the Target'. Entry and exit polls were taken, and after everyone had spoken, Michael D.'s approval rating in the room skyrocketed by 18 per cent.

Sean Gallagher's stock dropped 10 points in that SpunOut exit poll, not aided by his assertion at one point that unemployment was a human rights issue. But back in the real world, a *Sunday Business Post* poll had put Sean Gallagher on 39 per cent, miles ahead of everyone else. Incredibly, he managed to do this just by saying 'BUSINESS!' every now and then.

Gallagher's anodyne 'Come Exist with Me in Ireland' message seemed to strike a chord, even if his central plan of being a business ambassador had as much to do with the presidency as WD40 does in making a pizza. Others, however, with increasingly sharp barbs, were aghast at the notion that an ex-Fianna Fáiler and member of their National Executive at the height of Boomtime could end up in the big house.

It came to a head at the final and three zillionth studio debate of the presidential season, on *The Frontline* with Pat Kenny. With only a handful of days to tumble Gallagher's massive lead in the polls, it fell to Martin McGuinness to square up and throw a haymaker in Gallagher's direction. McGuinness claimed that a man had called him (mobile technology having rendered darkened car parks obsolete for this kind of thing) and said Gallagher invited him to An Audience with Brian Cowen. He also said Gallagher showed up at the mystery man's place with a photograph of the event and collected a cheque for five grand. This, apart from indicating that the man really knows how to charge for a photo, was McGuinness' Exhibit A in Gallagher being up to his neck in Fianna Fáil shenanigans and what he called 'brown envelope culture'.

Gallagher tried to pivot off point, claiming he didn't remember, but McGuinness, at this point the only man who had any sense of what was about to go down, said to Gallagher, 'I would caution you, you're in very murky waters here,' the camera cutting to people in the audience going, 'Ooh, this is class, isn't it?'

A break followed, but Gallagher wasn't saved by the

bell. Pat Kenny reopened the debate by announcing that Martin McGuinness' official Twitter page (it wasn't actually his account, but more on that anon) was indeed going to name the man in question (later revealed to be Hugh Morgan of Armagh jersey sponsorship fame, not of Fun Lovin' Criminals fame). Gallagher, *Ironside* theme apparently reverberating round in his head, scratched off his dignified veneer in dramatic fashion.

'I don't want to cast any aspersions', he started, '… but he's a convicted criminal, a fuel smuggler, was under investigation from the Criminal Assets Bureau and rented office space for Gerry Adams in the last election … I don't want to get involved in this.'

When Pat Kenny pressed him on why, given this man's roguish past, he invited him to a Fianna Fáil do in the first place, or if he'd had in fact received a cheque, Gallagher replied with the worst two possible words someone trying to distance themselves from Fianna Fáil could say: 'No recollection.' The crowd burst with rabble. And then …

'I may well have delivered the photograph, if he gave me an envelope … the point is, if he gave me a cheque, it was made out to Fianna Fáil headquarters.'

Wow. First of all, how can you be sure about the address on a cheque he wasn't even sure *existed*? Secondly, ENVELOPE? Who the hell mentioned anything about an envelope?

Having regurgitated the Fianna Fáil crony phrasebook

the night before, Gallagher cancelled his campaigning schedule to go on an explaining exercise that Tuesday. As if that wasn't mistake enough, on *Today with Pat Kenny* he tore into Glenna Lynch, an audience member who had effectively put Gallagher on the rack on *The Frontline* about his business practices and acumen.

'Who was the business woman and what was her background? And where does she come from and what party does she belong to, Pat? I'm tired of people being wheeled out with agendas,' Gallagher fulminated.

What he didn't realise was that she was driving in her car at the time, and pulled over to call in and jar him:

'It's absolutely shocking. I'm a completely normal person. I'm not involved in any political party. I think it is extraordinary that Sean believes that normal voters don't have a right to ask a question.'

Sean was never heard of again.

Well, strictly speaking that's not true. He has resurfaced sporadically with his lawsuit against RTÉ for the rogue tweet Pat Kenny erroneously claimed was from McGuinness' Twitter account, the tweet that he reckons lost him the election.

In the end, Michael D. became the first 'million vote candidate' after three counts, and the world news media responded with headlines like 'Elderly poet wins Irish Presidency'. That's President Elderly Poet to you, buddy.

❖

Perpetual Embarrassment Rating: 10/10
Gay Mitchell. Just, Gay Mitchell.

National Peril-o-meter: 7/10
National peril, not exactly, but nearly everybody lost a substantial amount of their soul in this election, one way or another.

'Ah, lads!' Rating: 10/10
We were one debate away from having Sean Gallagher as President. By quite a margin. Let's all sit back and ponder that quietly for a while.

Dana's preferred method of transport since the campaign:
Tank.

What Have We Learned?

Irish politicians should just not drink, ever:
Whether it's getting into their car and falling foul of the police, or politicians suggesting the police don't go too hard on the people who are, Irish politicians and alcohol is a dangerous cocktail. E*ven more* dangerous than a Jägerbomb. And by the way ...

It'd be a lot better if every TD had their *chauffeur:*
Imagine the scandal we'd save ourselves if TDs were *just driven* everywhere? No being stopped by the guards, no penalty points, no driving down places you're not supposed to drive down ...

Some politicians should never be allowed anywhere near a microphone:
Looking at y*ou, Ned O*'Keeffe. And Darren Scully. And Declan Ganley. And Paul Gogarty. And Gay Mitchell ... and so forth.

Irish politicians have a knack for getting a job they're either comically unqualified for or getting embroiled in a disaster oddly job-appropriate:

Science ministers endorsing anti-evolution books, Environment ministers wrecking all in front of them, Defence ministers flailing weaponry around, Transport ministers getting motoring fundamentally wrong, Finance ministers not having bank accounts; it's like cabinet appointments are made based on who's most likely to fatefully mess up.

The Irish populace are either incredibly sanguine or complete walkovers:

Other countries may be nipping at our heels political madness-wise, but on one specific thing we are without parallel: letting miscreants, scamps and full-on reprobates off the hook.

Irish politics is abjectly and peerlessly bonkers:

If the last few hundred pages have proved anything at all, it's this. As the old saying goes, 'Sure where would ye get it?'

Glossary

Maybe you don't keep up with Irish politics and could do with a refresher of the basics. Maybe you're not from Ireland and think Pee Flynn is some kind of vegetable pastry. Maybe you're of *Irish descent* and you're reading up on your crazy, crazy homeland. Maybe you found this book in a post-apocalyptic skip along with a packet of miraculously intact Cadbury's *Mini Rolls, and* are using both as the basis for A Glorious New Civilisation. Whatever the circumstances, it's always useful to be *able* to reference back on the oft-referenced people, roles and situations of Irish politics, so this helpful guide may, eh, help you.

- *The Dáil*: A centre for juvenile delinquency that seri*ously got ou*t of hand on Dublin's southside.
- *The Seanad*: I'll let you know as soon as I can figure it out.
- *The Oireachtas*: The collective term for the Dáil and

Seanad; I personally prefer 'A Murder of Dáil and Seanad'. You know, like crows.

- TD: A member of the Irish parliament, the TD stands for 'Tiresome druid'. I think.

- Taoiseach: The Prime Minister. As high as you can go in Irish politics, after that it's either retirement or a post in Europe. Or extended legal proceedings.

- Tánaiste: Deputy to the Taoiseach. In a coalition government, the Tánaiste is usually the leader of the party that will be destroyed at the next election.

- Ceann Comhairle: Speaker of the House. The best job in the Dáil, as they get to wear robes and ring a bell whenever they want and don't really have to listen to anything.

- Áras an Uachtaráin: The presidential residence. A house about seven or eight, to use the Fresh Prince system of domestic appraisal.

- Árd Fheis: A party convention. From the Irish words 'árd', meaning 'high', and 'feis', meaning 'an excuse for precocious children to get up in front of a large group of people and show off'.

- Fianna Fáil: Not so much a party as a way of life. Largely responsible for the current system of governance whereby TDs act like a guy who can get you smokes in prison.

- *Fine Gael*: A party known mainly for two things: Michael Collins and a brief flirtation with fascism. The most recent of these things happened 80 years ago, which tells you everything you need to know.

- *Labour*: Founded in 1913 by James Connolly, and a posthumous disappointment to him since 1916.

- *Sinn Féin*: A political party that used to believe in a ballot box in one hand and an Armalite in the other. They now use both their hands in the same way all the other political parties do: for excessive hand-gesturing.

- *DUP*: A hardline unionist party that would probably hate the very idea of being included in a glossary of Irish politics like this.

- *Seanie FitzPatrick*: You know Shere Khan in *The Jungle Book*? The banking equivalent of that, basically.

- *NAMA*: A bid to consolidate our financial woes into one manageable asset management agency. Stands for 'Negligible Affect, Monetary Assache'.

- *GUBU*: An acronym, 'Grotesque, Unbelievable, Bizarre, Unprecedented', describing the case of a double murderer hiding out in the Attorney General's house. The term became associated with Haughey's blisteringly mental government of 1982, and in later years has since been used as a catch-all term for things that are grotesque and bizarre, but far from unbelievable or unprecedented.

- *Fidelma Healy Eames*: A robot sent back in time from the future to permanently destroy the credibility of the Seanad.

- *Ronan Mullen*: The greatest Prime Minister the 1950s never had.

Did That Actually Happen?

- *David Norris*: Scholar, human rights activist and *Brideshead Revisited* character. A fan of straight talking, as long as you're talking from above the waist.
- *Donie Cassidy*: The Brian Epstein of music to put your wellies on to, later an influential senator.
- *Martin McGuinness*: Derry man, always good for a one-liner or ending a presidential rival's campaign. Ex-IRA, then NI MP and MLA for SF. Also, acronym hunter.
- *Gerry Adams*: Sinn Féin leader and most famous facial hair and glasses combo since Groucho Marx.
- *Charles Haughey*: A mythological creature invented by parents to scare children into lives of fiscal probity.
- *Michael Lowry*: What Peter Mandelson would have become had New Labour booted him out around 1996.
- *Pádraig 'Pee' Flynn*: A former cabinet minister and Mayo man with an ego so large it should have its own region on the *Shipping Forecast*.
- *Willie O'Dea*: A former cabinet minister who gives off the sense he missed his vocation as a traffic warden.
- *Paul Gogarty*: Green Party TD, fond of the F word. The last angry man in politics. No, seriously, he lost his seat in 2011.
- *The Healy-Raes*: In a land of blind men, the one-eyed man is King. In a land of Kerry men, the goat at the Killorglin Puck Fair is King, and the Healy-Raes are their public representatives.

Acknowledgements

A huge thank you to all the people who have helped me while writing this book. You know who you are.

But since that's a massive cop out, I will also let you know who they are. (This may take a while but feck it, it's me first book, ya know?)

Thanks to my editor Ciara Considine for her frankly absurd faith in me to undertake a project like this in the first place, and to all the Hachette Ireland team for making this such a tremendous and stress-free experience. Thanks to Tom Donnelly for his long-time guidance and his team on RTÉ's *Drivetime* for having a similarly absurd faith in me to do radio columns on air, without which Ciara would never have heard me or asked me to write the book, which would have rendered this page narcissistic madness.

And thanks to Ireland's politicians and the media who cover them, without whom I would have had no material whatsoever.

Thanks to everyone working on *University Challenge*

for being so supportive and encouraging about writing the book (which for a time amounted to my night job), and special thanks to Peter Gwyn and Steph Knight for their wise counsel, and Irene Daniels, Tom Benson and Vicki Smith for their relentless encouragement. Thanks also to the make-up ladies Kate and Julia who told Jeremy Paxman, who was incredibly generous in his congratulations and advice. Thanks to Ryan Tubridy for, as he always does, politely giving up his time to reply to a panicked email I sent him when it finally sank through that I was actually writing a book that other people would read. And thanks for him actually reading it too, and very generously letting me use his reaction on the cover. Thanks also to my editors at *The Huffington Post* and Kate Hickey from Irish Central for taking such a liberal attitude to my leaves of absence.

Thanks to all my dear friends, both at home and abroad, for their enduring support. Only for my natural sure-footedness and sturdy frame, I'd have been repeatedly bowled over by their kindness of thought and deed. Special mentions of thanks go to the following: to Andrew Gibbons, my long-time friend and collaborator over the years, and generally my first text when I see something insane in the news. The ideas for this book have in essence been forged in the hearth fire of our discussions over the years. To Kevin Ward, for regularly filling in for me on my journalistic pursuits, for his advice and always being inspiringly droll. To Mike Spring, for his searing genius, wisdom and mastery of puns. To Liz Mitchell, my international advisor of sorts (Birmingham counts as international, right?), for her invaluable counsel and for many times being a one-woman morale boost. To Ronan Gildea, who made sure my Donegal-themed reports were up to scratch. To Orla Tinsley, for her advice, generosity and generally being the most badass woman I know. And to Cara Ballingall. Just, in general.

Thanks also to Kenny Duffy (no relation – except perhaps in a cosmic sense) for sharing my excitement that I was being signed to the same publishing house as Michael Bolton. Thanks to Ed Woudhuysen for his suggestion that I include more Alan Partridge references in this book. Needless to say, I'll have the last laugh. And thanks to my best friend of ten years' standing Ray Gilger, for being the consistent butt of my jokes. I hope he's cool with the fact that this now counts as his next birthday and Christmas present. The dedication, that is. He'll have to buy the book himself.

To that end thanks to the wonderfully generous Breslin family of Bundoran, Thomas, Geraldine and my long-term friends Rachel and Susanna, who have all but pledged to dispense a warehouse full of these as Christmas presents. Thanks to John and Imelda Tierney from Headford whom I met at the breakfast table at a B&B outside Athlone, who told me the last person they'd met from Donegal was writing a book. I hadn't told them of my own at this point, so apart from being very nice people are obviously some kind of literary talisman.

A big thanks to Biljana Ljubjic and Matteo De Simone, Italian friends with whom I once had a discussion about which of our countries had the most embarrassing politicians. That conversation was the inspiration for the radio column that inspired the book, so I owe them quite a bit. Thanks also to my continental friends Charlotte Klein, Kian Badrnejad, Bojana Perisic and Patricia Tortosa for showing a truly heartening interest in the subject of what for them could have been a very esoteric book, and providing me with some uproarious anecdotes about their own national politics. Thanks to Nicola Connolly for her support and being consistently as excited over the years as I am when I get to do fun stuff like this. And thanks to Siobhan Walsh, a real oasis of calm, ever-serene wisdom and knowledge.

Thanks to *Reeling in the Years*. It really is a top programme.

A special thanks too to everyone I've worked with in the youth advocacy sector, especially to all at SpunOut.ie and the Donegal Youth Council. Those two organisations, and the people who have made them what they are, fill me with immeasurable pride.

And thanks to my mentors without whom my professional career would be a shapeless husk, and whose example I always try to follow: to Janet Gaynor, Ruairi McKiernan and Angie Ryan.

And speaking of examples to follow, last but never

least, thanks to my family, Margaret, Paddy and Oisín Duffy, for their love, generosity, humour and perpetual patience. Without them not just humouring but encouraging my constant questions and chatter from Day One, keeping me stocked in atlases and encyclopaedias and continuously going out of their way to make sure I could find mine, there is no godly way any of this would be possible. I'll never be able to repay that. But who knows, maybe the royalties for this book will make a bit of a dent, eh?!

And thanks to my late Uncle Philsy Grogan, a lifelong role model and a man who truly knew something about doing the State some service.

Also can you play 'Real Gone Kid' by Deacon Blue for Tom and Josephine's twenty-fifth wedding anniversary tomorrow, love from Big John and the family. Sorry, can someone give that one to Larry Gogan?